HUMAN LIFE PRIORITY

Human Life Priority

Yunus Ciptawilangga, M.B.A.

Elm Hill

A Division of
HarperCollins Christian Publishing

www.elmhillbooks.com

Human Life Priority

Published in Nashville, Tennessee, by Elm Hill, an imprint of Thomas Nelson. Elm Hill and Thomas Nelson are registered trademarks of HarperCollins Christian Publishing, Inc.

Elm Hill titles may be purchased in bulk for educational, business, fund-raising, or sales promotional use. For information, please e-mail SpecialMarkets@ThomasNelson.com.

Library of Congress Cataloging-in-Publication Data

Library of Congress Control Number: 2020904508

ISBN 978-1-400330522 (Paperback)
ISBN 978-1-400330539 (eBook)

Foreword

I do not know how you become a Christian. I have been to Sunday school since childhood and was baptized when I was a teen. But in 1980 when I lectured in my first year, I got a course "comparative study of religions" where the subject made me realize that religion is not only Christian, but there are still four other major religions besides several other religions. Since then, I began to learn the five religions, namely, Hinduism, Buddhism, Islam, Catholicism, and Christianity.

In the year of 2000, I did wholeheartedly choose to become a follower of Christ after understanding and believing that salvation only exists in and through Jesus Christ. During the twenty years of learning these five religions, I did not leave Christianity but refused to be active and take ecclesiastical ministry. During this period at least twice I was offered to run for deacon, but I was not willing and only willing to be a guest greeter twice in one year. Why? Because at that time, I was still not sure that I would still be a Christian. I did not want to cause a stir when I later move to become a follower of another religion.

After fully being a follower of Christ, I am serious enough to study and practice my beliefs. I began to diligently read the Bible, pray regularly every midnight, and try to do God's Word. I am also quite diligent in listening to recorded sermons from many servants of God.

In late 2006 when in a meeting with my professionals, I said that later each person would have a chip planted in his hand or forehead, and my information technology manager said that it had been done in several countries. I was quite surprised, and after studying the data presented by the manager, I began to explore the material of the end times.

In 2009 I found strong evidence that we are in the last days, so in 2010, I sold most of my business and began to study end times more seriously and to engage in service. Praise God, since 2013 with two other writers, namely, Rev. Jopie Rattu, PhD, and Mr. Sridadi Atiyanto, PhD, I managed to write six books of the end times which were later merged into two books with the title *The Rapture, the Fulfillment of: The Signs in the Sky, the Festivals in Summer, and the Parable of the End Times* Part I and Part II and published by HarperCollins.

In addition to writing end-time books, I also wrote as many as thirty thin books derived from the material of my sermon which was then made into four books consisting of a combination of seven to eight thin books.

The four books each take one of the book titles as the combined title of the book.

The first book is entitled *Human Life Priority* which consists of eight books, where other books are *The Value of Salvation*, *The Rights and Responsibilities of God's Children*, *The Foundations of Christianity*, *The Characteristics of Children of God*, *Four Types of Christians*, *Jesus Versus Mammon*, and *The Great Commission*.

The second book is entitled *The Blessed Christian Family* which consists of seven books, where other books are *Family Worship*, *The Major Ministry*, *Blessing*, *Our Attitude in the House of God*, *Worship the Father in Spirit and in Truth*, and *To Be Children of God or Servants of God*.

The third book is entitled *Becoming a Fruitful People of God* which consists of seven books, where other books are *The Fruit of the Spirit, Victorious People, Be Converted and Become as Little Children, Our Speech, Joy,* and *Main Duties of a Servant of God.*

The fourth book is entitled *Faith and Deeds* which consists of eight books, where other books are *Five Foolish Virgins and Wise Ones, God's Promise to Provide, Heaviest Temptations, A People Prepared for the Lord, To Do the Will of the Father, Loving God,* and *Give Glory unto the Lord.*

Most readers like these books because they are thin, so they can be read on a trip or while they are waiting because they are generally finished in twenty to thirty minutes. Other than that, the books are also easy to understand because they are simply explained with examples and written in simple language. Even so, each topic was discussed in sufficient depth accompanied by supporting verses.

Besides these books are also in demand by pastors and servants of God because these books come from sermon material so that they can deliver the contents of the book in the form of sermons.

Praise God the Lord, although I have never been to theological school, I was given an understanding of these topics according to the Word of God recorded in Matthew 7:7:

> *Ask and it will be given to you; seek and you will find; knock and the door will be opened to you.*

In fact, every child of God can not only understand God's Words, they can even know about God our Father to the deep things, as written in 1 Corinthians 2:10:

these are the things God has revealed to us by his Spirit. The Spirit searches all things, even the deep things of God.

In closing I would like to say a big thanks to a senior pastor who does not want to be named who helped to correct and give input to almost all books that I wrote.

Soli Deo Gloria,
Yunus Ciptawilangga

HUMAN
LIFE
PRIORITY
MONEY
FAMILY
RELIGION
SOCIAL
Yunus Ciptawilangga, MBA

HUMAN LIFE PRIORITY

The writer does not know whether the reader has experienced what often disturbed the writer's mind especially when he is attending a funeral.

When the writer comes to a funeral, a question would often pop up: "Actually, what is a human being's main task in this life?" This thought becomes stronger as the writer joins in the procession of bringing the deceased to the cemetery with another thought: "If there was a major task that this person had to perform in his/her life, had this deceased person done his/her major task?"

The writer believes that there must be a task that is already planned by God for human beings to perform while living in the world, besides secondary things. This thought came up when the writer remembered the security guards in his house. The writer often sees them help in watering the plants in the morning and in the afternoon. The plants grow well, but still, should one day the house got burgled, the writer will reprimand or even dismiss them because they neglected their primary duty, which is to maintain security of the house.

Likewise, with our lives, we may have and do a lot of sideline activities, but we still have a major task as human beings created by God in His image and likeness. And it turned out that what was thought over by the writer has also been thought over by Solomon and discussed in the book of Ecclesiastes. So, we will discuss and contemplate on the book of Ecclesiastes.

Ecclesiastes 1:1 The words of the Teacher, son of David, king in Jerusalem:

This was Solomon's words and then subsequently in Ecclesiastes 2:3, he said:

*I tried cheering myself with wine, and embracing **folly**—my mind still guiding me with wisdom. I wanted to see what was good for people to do under the heavens during the few days of their lives.*

This verse explained that Solomon really wanted to know what was best done by human beings in their lives in the world or what in fact the priority of human life was. Solomon's seriousness in investigating the matter was described in Ecclesiastes 2:3 where Solomon exercised his wisdom and drank wine to refresh himself and insisted on or continued to study like a fool until he knew what the priority of human life was that must be done during his short life in this world.

Wealth, Throne, and Women

Many people assume that a person is considered successful if he possesses three things, namely, wealth, throne, and women. That is why many people are focused on attaining these things. They consider having wealth, throne or position, and women as the priority of human life.

If we study the book of Ecclesiastes, we will see that Solomon did that, too.

Let's study together to see what Solomon's opinions and experiences about wealth, throne, and women were.

Wealth

As a king, Solomon's wealth was incredibly abundant; he was continually collecting wealth that he became the richest man in his era.

Ecclesiastes 2:7 says:

I bought male and female slaves and had other slaves who were born in my house. I also ***owned more herds and flocks than anyone in Jerusalem before me****.*

Solomon not only collected gold and silver, but he also collected art objects as described in Ecclesiastes 2:8a:

I amassed silver and gold for myself, and the treasure of kings and provinces.

But after becoming the richest man, Solomon realized that all attempts to collect wealth will be inexhaustible, without end, and finally in Ecclesiastes 5:10, he said:

Whoever loves money never has enough; whoever loves wealth is never satisfied with their income. This too is meaningless.

So, after collecting treasures as much as it was, he finally said, "This is also meaningless." Why was treasure meaningless?

> *As goods increase, so do those who consume them. And what benefit are they to the owners except to feast their eyes on them?*
>
> *(ECCLESIASTES 5:11)*

Having many possessions is also vanity because other people will consume them. We can only eat as much as one plate every time we dine, and we sleep in one bed, and even if we have fifty houses, we can only inhabit one house at a time. In fact, he said in Ecclesiastes 5:12:

> *The sleep of a labouring man is sweet, whether he eat little or much: but the abundance of the rich will not suffer him to sleep.*

Even poor people sleep better than rich people who eat until satiated.

Solomon continued:

> *I have seen a grievous evil under the sun: wealth hoarded to the harm of its owners.*
>
> *(ECCLESIASTES 5:13)*

In fact, many wealthy people experienced disaster because of their wealth, whether they were attacked, robbed, or abducted or their children fighting over the inheritance or even killed each other.

Solomon also realized that a person's wealth can be gone instantly when struck by misfortune, such as natural disaster, financial crisis, war, or other calamities. Apparently, all the wealth that had been boasted of as enough for seven generations of offspring were used up so that nothing can be inherited even for his son.

> *...or wealth lost through some misfortune, so that when they have children there is nothing left for them to inherit.*
>
> *(ECCLESIASTES 5: 14)*

Solomon concluded his opinion about wealth by saying that even if a person has an abundance of riches, upon death, he will not be able to bring his property along.

> *Everyone comes naked from their mother's womb, and as everyone comes, so they depart. They take nothing from their toil that they can carry in their hands.*
>
> *(ECCLESIASTES 5:15)*

> *This too is a grievous evil: As everyone comes, so they depart, and what do they gain, since they toil for the wind?*
>
> *(ECCLESIASTES 5:16)*

Throne

Throne or position causes a person to gain power. His words became influential; with his position, he could command many things. Position causes a person to be respected and even feared. He lives like a god who can do anything. A king could even make a decree to revoke a person's life. Therefore, many people fight to sit on a throne or get a position because then he will become a powerful person.

Solomon was one of Israel's greatest kings, as noted in the following verses:

So King Solomon ruled over all Israel.

(1 KINGS 4:1)

And Solomon ruled over all the kingdoms from the Euphrates River to the land of the Philistines, as far as the border of Egypt. These countries brought tribute and were Solomon's subjects all his life.

(1 KINGS 4:21)

What was Solomon's comment about his throne?

I hated all the things I had toiled for under the sun, because I must leave them to the one who comes after me.

(ECCLESIASTES 2:18)

And who knows whether ***that person will be wise or foolish****? Yet they will have control over all the fruit of my toil into which I have poured my effort and skill under the sun. This too is meaningless.*

(ECCLESIASTES 2:19)

Solomon said that all his efforts to become a great king were vanity because when he passed away, he had to leave everything to the next king whose competence he did not know.

And what Solomon feared really happened in his life. We know that Solomon built a huge empire, but not until a month after his son inherited it, the kingdom was divided. When his son, Rehoboam, followed the advice of his peers over the counsel of the elders, the Israelites rebelled so that the kingdom was split into two.

Women

Treasure, throne, and women are an inseparable package. A man who has considerable wealth may have several wives, especially if he rules over a country as a king with absolute power. In ancient times, a king could have hundreds of wives and concubines, but even in this modern age, there are still people who practice polygamy.

Solomon said in Ecclesiastes 2:8b:

> *I acquired male and female singers, and* ***a harem*** *as well—the delights of a man's heart.*

1 Kings 11:3a says that Solomon had seven hundred wives from noble backgrounds and three hundred concubines.

Later, Solomon realized that having many wives did not make him better because his wives made him follow God half-heartedly, and in his old age, Solomon even turned away his heart from God and after other gods worshipped by his wives because they had influenced his belief.

That explained why he wrote the following:

> *I find more bitter than death the woman who is a snare, whose heart is a trap and whose hands are chains. The man who pleases God will escape her, but the sinner she will ensnare.*
>
> *(Ecclesiastes 7:26)*

Wisdom

Besides seeking treasure, throne, and women, Solomon also studied a lot to gain a lot of knowledge because he viewed wisdom or knowledge as most important in human life.

> *I saw that wisdom is better than folly, just as light is better than darkness.*
>
> *(ECCLESIASTES 2:13)*

> *The wise have eyes in their heads, while the fool walks in the darkness.*
>
> *(ECCLESIASTES 2:14A)*

At first Solomon thought that wise people were extraordinary people who could discern right from wrong and give fair consideration, as opposed to fools who walked in darkness.

> *He spoke three thousand proverbs and his songs numbered a thousand and five.*
>
> *(1 KINGS 4:32)*

> *He spoke about plant life, from the cedar of Lebanon to the hyssop that grows out of walls. He also spoke about animals and birds, reptiles and fish.*
>
> *(1 KINGS 4:33)*

Solomon spoke 3,000 proverbs and composed 1,005 songs. He spoke of trees: from the cedar trees on Mount Lebanon to the hyssop that grew on the walls. (Hyssop was a small plant whose stems and leaves could be used to sprinkle liquid). He also had extensive knowledge about animals, birds, reptiles, and fish. How amazing! He studied everything.

But then he said that having a lot of knowledge was also useless because everyone would surely die, both foolish and wise men.

> *Then I said to myself, "The fate of the fool will overtake me also. What then do I gain by being wise?" I said to myself, "This too is meaningless."*
>
> *(ECCLESIASTES 2:15)*

Besides this, Solomon also realized that even a wise person would still be subjected to calamities that can occur and befall on everyone, both the fool and the smart.

A man's fate is in God's hands and he cannot control it; for example, when Aceh or Japan was struck by a severe tsunami, everyone—whether smart, stupid, and low or highly educated—cannot be spared from death.

> *Moreover, no one knows when their hour will come: As fish are caught in a cruel net, or birds are taken in a snare, so people are trapped by evil times that fall unexpectedly upon them.*
>
> *(ECCLESIASTES 9:12)*

Furthermore, there were other things that were unattainable by human wisdom since there were other powers that controlled and regulated human life.

> *I have seen something else under the sun: The race is not to the swift or the battle to the strong, nor does food come to the wise or wealth to the brilliant or favor to the learned; but time and chance happen to them all.*
>
> *(ECCLESIASTES 9:11)*

When we look around, we will notice that many things happen not in accordance with the laws of nature. The fast will not always win a race, the strong will not always be superior, and the rich—whose diet is more nutritious—will not necessarily be wiser than the poor. The intelligent people are not necessarily richer and the smart and educated may not necessarily receive the grace of God because there are situations that are beyond the control of man, namely, time and fate that have been appointed by God to every human being.

Solomon continued:

> *For the wise, like the fool, will not be long remembered; the days have already come when both have been forgotten. Like the fool, the wise too must die!*
>
> *(ECCLESIASTES 2:16)*

The wise man will also die. Even if he has done a phenomenal work, still in the long run, he will be forgotten. For example, do you know who Edward Jenner was? We still use his research results until this time. As children, we have all been vaccinated against chicken pox, haven't we? And Edward Jenner was the inventor, but how many of us still remember him? Almost none, although we had used and enjoyed the benefits of his research. He had spent a lot of time studying and conducting his research and made a great deal of sacrifice, but unfortunately, we did not know him and even forget him.

If all human efforts, such as collecting treasure, occupying the throne, having many wives, and even searching for wisdom, are useless, what should we do in this life? Let us go back to our initial topic: what is exactly the priority of human life?

At the end of the closing chapters, Solomon said:

> *Now all has been heard; here is the conclusion of the matter:* ***Fear God and keep his commandments****, for* ***this is the duty of all mankind****.*
>
> *(ECCLESIASTES 12:13)*

> *For* ***God will bring every deed into judgment****, including every hidden thing,* ***whether it is good or evil****.*
>
> *(ECCLESIASTES 12:14)*

The closing verses will be easier to understand if we read verse 14 first and then read verse 13. All men will be judged by God for all his deeds, whether good or bad. So, we have to prepare ourselves to face that court. And the preparation is by becoming a person who fears God and keeps all His commandments.

Twenty Years of Seeking for the True Religion

As mentioned in his book, the writer was allowed by God to seek for the true religion for twenty years. The writer had been attending Sunday school since childhood and had been baptized in his teens.

When he was in his first year of college, he took a comparative religious studies course. The course made him aware that in this world, not only the Christian religion existed, but there were four other religions. From that course he studied the five religions, and in year 2000, with full conviction, he wholeheartedly made a firm decision to be a follower of Christ.

Once, while he was telling his experience, one listener commented that if the writer had not spent so much time in studying religion, he might have become richer than he was then. The opinion might be true, but the writer never regretted the time he had spent because seeking for the true religion and following it is a major priority of man's life.

Conclusion

Humans are triune creatures, composed of body, soul, and spirit. The body is physical, which we can see and touch. The soul or the life God breathed into man's nostrils is the element that distinguishes between people who are still alive and people who are dead; therefore a dead man is often referred to as a body devoid of life. On the other hand, a person who is mentally ill is a person whose spirit is sick, although physically he is fit enough. Unlike the body that is physical, the soul and the spirit are immaterial. From the above explanation, we understand that man is a spirit that has a soul in a body.

Basically, all religions believe in three things, namely, as follows:

First, the body is temporary, but the spirit is immortal.

Second, there is life after death.

Third, there is the final judgment that will determine whether our spirit will live in a good place (heaven), which gives happiness forever, or stay in a terrible place (hell), where our spirits will be tormented forever.

The priority of human life is to prepare ourselves so that later we go to heaven; that is the first and most important thing.

Every religion teaches ways to get to heaven, but Christianity explains that only in Christ there is a guarantee of salvation; in that we are granted the right to enter heaven by accepting Jesus as Lord and Savior, as written in the following:

> *Jesus answered, "I am the way and the truth and the life. No one comes to the Father except through me."*
>
> *(JOHN 14:6)*

> *Salvation is found in no one else, for there is no other name under heaven given to mankind by which we must be saved.*
>
> *(ACTS 4:12)*

To enter heaven is the priority of human life. Our priority is not to make money as much as possible, not to occupy a position as high as possible, not have wives as many as possible, and not study to earn a degree as high as possible, but to prepare ourselves and make sure that we shall go to heaven.

The Value of Salvation

Yunus Ciptawilangga, MBA

The Value of Salvation

Preface

Nowadays we often hear and see many of God's children falling away; they give up or leave their faith and become followers of another religion due to persecutions, positions, wealth, life partner, and so on.

If we observe more closely, one of the main reasons they are willing to give up their faith is because they do not know or realize how invaluable the salvation they have gained when they accept Jesus Christ as their Lord and Savior. Therefore, as God's children, we need to study and ponder on the real value of this salvation God has bestowed on us so that we would keep, maintain, and treasure our salvation.

The Lord Jesus made it clear that in the end times, many of God's children would turn away from their faith and become apostates:

> *At that time many will turn away from the faith and will betray and hate each other.*
>
> (Matthew 24:10)

Therefore, today we should be more serious in studying and doing the Word so that we would have a solid foundation as our base to strengthen our faith and be able to remain faithful in following the Lord as long as we live, until the end.

> *For this very reason, make every effort to add to your faith goodness; and to goodness, **knowledge**.*
>
> *(2 PETER 1:5)*

Soli Deo Gloria,
The writer

The Value of Salvation

As a Christian the writer is convinced that we all believe God is righteous and just. However, still many are somewhat confused to see the situations and facts around us, even what are happening today in our lives, and wonder what God's justice is really like.

Oftentimes contradictory matters are confronted with the concept that God is righteous and just. For example, many people think that since God is righteous and just, "Why am I not created as pretty as A or as handsome as B?" Some also comment that if God is righteous and just, "Why is my health not as good as others', or why was I not born into a rich family, or why am I not as fortunate as others," and so on.

Examples of such confusion could disseminate or spread to other areas, such as convenience or welfare, struggles of life, housing, employment, and many others.

Where Is God's Righteousness and Justice?

Actually, many people not only do not understand how the Lord God acts in His righteousness and justice; in fact they still question whether He is truly righteous and just. If God is righteous and just, why don't I experience the effects of that? As human beings, are we not equally created by God? Then why should we receive different treatments and fates?

A Father and His Four Daughters

There was a father who had four daughters. The father wanted to give them gifts. Each child would get a box with the same kind of present, which was to be placed on the left side, but each of them would also obtain a different additional gift. So, each of them would receive a similar present added with a different one.

The youngest daughter got a present plus a twenty grams gold necklace. The third daughter was given a similar present plus a ten grams gold bracelet. The second daughter was given a similar present plus a five grams gold ring, while the firstborn daughter was given a similar present plus a piece of plastic clip.

Do you think this man as a father had treated his daughters righteously or justly? In general, we may consider this unfair or unjust. Why was one given an additional present of a twenty grams gold necklace, the other one a ten grams gold bracelet, then the next one a five grams gold ring, while the eldest only a piece of plastic clip?

In this case, the father's fairness or justice can only be understood once we know for certain what was in the box of the main present, *which each of the four daughters received equally.* If the content of the box was a twenty carats good-quality diamond, surely the addition of a twenty grams gold necklace, or a ten grams gold bracelet, or a five grams gold ring, or even a simple plastic clip to such a precious gift would hardly make any difference since the price of a flawless D color diamond as big as twenty carats could reach five million USD.

If the price of gold is fifty USD per gram, then twenty grams of gold would be equal to one thousand USD. So, the total price obtained by those children respectively would be five million and one thousand, five million and five hundred, five million and two hundred and fifty and five million only, which virtually were of no significant difference. Why? Gold would lose its value because the value is too small compared with the value of the diamond, especially if the gifts were of a grand size bigger than 100 carats, with an estimation over 100 million USD. Thus, gold of 250–1,000 was considered insignificant.

Passing from Hell to Heaven

Likewise, when we receive salvation, we will enter the Kingdom of Heaven, and this is something so amazing and wonderful that all wealth and other prosperous conditions we are in would become insignificant, something of no value at all. Through the redemption by the Lord Jesus Christ, we are removed or transferred from hell, and not only transferred or redeemed from hell, but we would go into heaven.

Because of sin, we are separated from God and condemned to go into hell. However, by the death of Jesus Christ, we are redeemed from being sent to hell and even granted eternal life in heaven. From being condemned to live in hell forever, we are ransomed and changed to being blessed and then enter the heaven to live there forever.

Differences Between Prison and Hell

Many people today who are facing a lawsuit are prosecuted for a certain offense. They fought desperately and engaged the best lawyers, making the best efforts so as not to be put behind the bars. But what if being put in jail is compared with being sent to hell? So very different, isn't it? Like heaven and earth. Let's say that someone is imprisoned for five to ten years or even for life. He would endure it at the most for a few decades only, whereas if we go to hell, we would be punished and tortured forever as described in the following verse:

And throw that worthless servant outside, into the darkness, where there will be weeping and gnashing of teeth.

(MATTHEW 25:30)

...where "the worms that eat them do not die, and the fire is not quenched."

(MARK 9:48)

To be sent to hell would last forever and ever, being tortured continuously. Life in prison may be difficult, but not tortured all the times. In hell the torture goes on and on, forever and terribly awful. But, on the contrary, if we may enter the heaven, what would we get there? We would be given joy forever, an eternal joy.

'He will wipe every tear from their eyes. There will be no more death' or mourning or crying or pain, for the old order of things has passed away.

(REVELATION 21:4)

Thus, the implied meaning of the value of salvation is that we are redeemed, saved from the eternal torment in hell, and we would be given eternal life full of joy in heaven.

Justice of God

Indeed, God offers salvation to *every human being*, without exception, to be received freely, as recorded in the following verse:

*For God so loved the world that he gave his one and only Son, that **whoever** believes in him shall not perish but have eternal life.*

(JOHN 3:16)

And as described previously, whenever we believe and accepted God's offered salvation which is so invaluable, of such an inestimable value, then other things become meaningless.

That's why when the Apostle Paul knew and experienced the love of God which is realized in the salvation through Jesus Christ, he stated:

What is more, I consider everything a loss because of the surpassing worth of knowing Christ Jesus my Lord, for whose sake I have lost all things. I consider them garbage, that I may gain Christ.

(PHILIPPIANS 3:8)

The Apostle Paul did not only state that other things, either wealth, worldly pleasures, honor, or other secular matters, are of no value at all; he even said that those things he counted but dung or trash compared to the salvation the Lord God had given him. Why as garbage? Because God's offered salvation through Jesus' sacrifice on the cross, for our redemption from hell (the eternal death), is incomparable!

The Millennium Kingdom of Christ and His Saints

When we study more deeply, in fact when we receive salvation through Jesus Christ, we are not only redeemed from hell and get the assurance to live eternally in heaven, but prior to it, we would join in the Millennium Kingdom (One Thousand Years Reign of Christ and His Saints). This is clearly recorded in the Book of Revelation that later, before entering into heaven, we would be (present) in the world for a thousand years.

Blessed and holy are those who share in the first resurrection. The second death has no power over them, but they will be ***priests of God*** *and of Christ and will* ***reign*** *with him for a thousand years.*

(REVELATION 20:6)

At that time we would be priests of God who offer praises to God. And besides, we would also reign with the Lord Jesus Christ and enjoy life in this world as kings.

Salvation Is a Gift by Grace

Many people, even Christians, underestimate the concept of salvation. Since salvation is a gift by grace, which can be obtained at no charge/ price, they often show indifference and *treat salvation as if it is something cheap* (unworthy or unimportant). Yet, if we but study more, this salvation is made possible because God redeemed mankind from the condemnation of their/our sins through Christ, by sacrificing Christ's own life. Now, since God redeemed us from our sins by the death of Christ, His Son, why should this salvation be given freely? Salvation is given freely not because it is so cheap but, on the contrary, because *salvation is so invaluable, so very expensive* that no man would be able to pay for it. Since no human being is able to pay for the sacrifice of the Lord Jesus, thus God bestows it as grace.

Back to the previous parable of the twenty carats diamond, actually one of the most expensive diamond these days is the Koh-I-Noor, the diamond sought and pursued by many and had consumed victims up to a few thousands, perhaps even tens of thousands people. This diamond is now mounted on the crown of the Queen of England. The price estimated is at around one billion USD, a very high price indeed. Although the diamond is so expensive, and let's say we have it, this very diamond would not pay for our salvation! And neither the richest man in the world today, Jeff Bezos, even with his fortune of one hundred and thirty billion dollars. If this whole wealth of one hundred and thirty billion dollars were offered to pay for this salvation, it too would be inadequate because we read in Matthew 16:26:

> *What good will it be for someone to gain the whole world, yet forfeit their soul? Or what can anyone give in exchange for their soul?*

Hence, even if someone gains the whole world, he still would not be capable to pay for his life. He would not be able to pay for his own salvation. These all show us how expensive the price of this eternal salvation is, so we can understand why the Lord grant it as His grace, since whatever we have and however expensive those are, there is nothing we can do to pay for this salvation.

If we understand and always bear in mind that salvation is so very expensive, then surely there is no one among us who will relinquish our salvation. No one will ever want to give it up just for the sake of either his/her spouse, position, or wealth, however much it is. Even persecuted, we will not let go of our salvation.

As children of God, we might bear the intention to hold fast our salvation; let's say we have promised to remain faithful to the Lord so that we would truly experience what the Apostle Paul expressed in 2 Timothy 4:7:

> *I have fought the good fight, I have finished the race, I have kept the faith.*

If such is our conviction, then it is indeed something good, even something that we must own. Yet James 2:14 says:

What good is it, my brothers and sisters, if someone claims to have faith but has no deeds? Can such faith save them?

The above verse explains that it is not enough when we express our faith merely by our speech or confession of belief. We must show it *in our actions* or conducts too as the manifestation of our faith. Have we taken actions as proof of our faith? Let us examine ourselves and find out whether each of us truly belongs to those who hold fast to our faith, by following these conducts:

First: Our prayer life

Let us compare ourselves with the followers of another religion. They pray five times a day, at the appointed times, starting at dawn. Besides that, they also have to follow the ritual to cleanse themselves before they pray.

We as Christians can pray at any time, and there are relatively no rituals to follow as they ought to. The question is: *how many times do we pray every day?*

Second: Read the Bible

Many followers of other religions diligently read their Sacred Books which are written in a language foreign to them. Hence to be able to understand, they must learn that foreign language. Yet even in such circumstance, they are determined to read the Book through and diligently do so.

Our Holy Bible is written in our national language, and we can also find some translations in our mother tongues. Communities in some areas, where they do not master the national language, can get a

Bible in their local languages. The question is: *how often do we read the Bible?* Now, until today in our lifetime or after so many years following Jesus Christ our Lord and Savior, how many times have we completed reading through the Bible, from the Book of Genesis to the Book of Revelation, while the language is easily understood?

Third: Worship faithfully

Some religions built their temples far up the hills. To go there they have to ascend many stairs provided, some a hundred, two hundred, three hundred, or more, up to a thousand steps. Some adherents of those religions even pray at every step before reaching the temple or the place of worship! Going up each step of the stairs, they would fall on their knees and pray and then rise up to ascend another step, kneel down again to pray, and so on. Thus, they have to go there very early in the morning, at dawn, and would reach the place of worship in the afternoon. Some are shielded by an umbrella and some reject any protection so that they would probably be burnt by the scorching sun and soaked by the rain. In fact some of them reject any kind of cover or cushion to protect their knees while praying, so after several times kneeling down to pray, their knees start bleeding.

Christianity does not teach us to do so. The regulations of our worship are simple: go in, sit down, and attend the worship. The question is: *How often and how seriously do we go into God's house?* Some people may be reluctant to go to church even when it rains but a little, or the traffic seemed to be jammed, or there are other programs or events more interesting and considered more important than to attend a worship service in the church.

Likewise, we should be concerned about our attitude as we worship. Let us take, for example, the community in Bali. Those who attend the worship are so serious. Wearing their best clothes, clad in very neat uniforms, they pray very solemnly. On the contrary, some of us are heard chatting, and some also eat and drink while attending the worship service in church.

Fourth: Sacrificing our wealth and future

The followers of some particular religion ought to make a pilgrimage to their Holy Land in order to consummate the requirements of their religion. To accomplish that journey, they have to plan the time well, learn and follow the procedures and regulations of worship prescribed, and of course also spend a huge cost. And we often hear that some of them have to sell their houses, rice fields, and precious possessions for the sake of completing those religious requirements.

Whereas we, at the most we are apt to give some money as an offering, put into the collecting bags or tray passed on during the worship service. *How much do we put therein* as an expression of our gratefulness for all God's provisions and blessings every day? And *do we remember to give our tithes too?*

Many young men in Thailand were willing to *give up all their possessions and their future to become monks*, who would live purely on the mercy of others in their whole life.

For what purpose do they do all those?

Basically they do all those *to obtain salvation*.

From us is required only our tithes, a ten percent of what we earn, meaning that we still have ninety percent left for us to keep, while the followers of that religion *sacrifice all their wealth and their future!*

However, when we talk about giving our tithes, it is not because God wants ten percent of our money. Let us observe the verse of Malachi 3:10,

> *"Bring the whole tithe into the storehouse, that there may be food in my house. Test me in this," says the Lord Almighty, "and see if I will not* ***throw open the floodgates of heaven and pour out so much blessing that there will not be room enough to store it.****"*

This verse above emphatically describes that the tithes are rendered not because God wants to take from us, but rather because *God wants to bless us abundantly!*

Do we faithfully obey to give our tithes?

Besides the tithes, we are also required to care and provide for our relatives as is written in 1 Timothy 5:8:

> *Anyone who does not provide for their relatives, and especially for their own household, has denied the faith and is worse than an unbeliever.*

God clearly commands us to help our kinsfolk or relatives. Do we do it?

James 2:26 says, "As the body without the spirit is dead, so *faith without deeds is dead.*"

Therefore, as God's children who have faith, who hold our salvation firmly, let us all take action as an obvious manifestation of our faith. Do not wait because time is very short.

The Rights and Responsibilities of God's Children

Yunus Ciptawilangga, MBA

The Rights and Responsibilities of God's Children

Preface

As Christians, we are God's children. However, though we consider ourselves as children of God and call God as our Father, actually we often assume those terms *children of God* and *Father* just as "titles," not as "status." Such an assumption basically becomes the reason why *we are less aware that we truly have the status or position as God's children.*

The lack or absence of the awareness about this status as children of God can be the cause why some Christians easily shunt their status as they do not realize what a grand gift they possess. So, when a Christian lacks the awareness concerning his or her status as God's child, the person would scarcely think about his/her rights and responsibilities or obligations.

This thin book is to explain, first, about how we may obtain the status as children of God and then, second, the rights we possess pertaining the status and the responsibilities or obligations thereof.

We would be overwhelmed when we know how wonderful the rights God gives us as His children. Therefore, let us study together about this most important issue while thanking our Heavenly Father for His grace to grant us the opportunity to understand this.

> *...these are the things God has revealed to us by his Spirit. The Spirit searches all things, even the deep things of God.*
>
> (I CORINTHIANS 2:10)

Soli Deo Gloria,
The writer

Becoming God's Children

Right away, when we accept Jesus Christ as our Lord and Savior, we will be saved. This is recorded among others in Romans 10:9:

> *If you* ***declare with your mouth, "Jesus is Lord,"*** *and* ***believe*** *in your heart that* ***God raised him from the dead****, you* ***will be saved****.*

As it is written in the verse, this belief should be uttered or pronounced by our own mouth. This utterance of our belief, or our confession of faith on how or why we receive Jesus Christ as our personal Lord and Savior, is usually done in the form of prayer, namely, *a prayer of acceptance or recognition*. And here is an example of such prayer on how we accept and recognize Jesus Christ as our Lord and Savior:

Lord Jesus, here I come to You. I confess that I am a sinner deserved to be punished. But now I believe that You have died to save sinners. Please come into my heart as my personal Lord and Savior. Forgive all my sins and please write my name in the book of life so that I belong to them who obtain eternal life. I believe that from now on, I have the assurance of salvation in the Kingdom of Heaven. In the name of the Lord Jesus, I pray gratefully. Hallelujah, amen.

This is just an example and does not always have to be the same, but the essence of the confession of faith is the same and does not change.

The Meaning of Baptism

Then the next process should be in accordance with the Great Commission as recorded in Matthew 28:19–20:

Therefore go and make disciples of all nations, ***baptizing*** *them in the name of the Father and of the Son and of the Holy Spirit.*

(Matthew 28:19)

...and teaching them to obey everything I have commanded you. And surely I am with you always, to the very end of the age.

(Matthew 28:20)

So, our confession should be followed by *baptism*, the sacrament through which we publicly declare our faith as followers of Christ, as God's children, before some people or an audience, such as servants of God or church congregation or both as witnesses.

Immersion Baptism and Sprinkling Baptism

Generally, there are two types of baptisms: the sprinkling baptism and the immersion baptism. The verb "to baptize" means "to immerse," from the Greek word *baptizo*, which means "plunging, dipping or soaking, ...washing" (*Bauer, Arndt, Gingrich, A Greek-English Lexicon of the New Testament and Other Early Christian Literature, 1952, p. 131*).

The writer personally believes that baptism by immersion is more appropriate because in addition to the meaning of the word *baptizo* above, the Lord Jesus Himself also was baptized by being immersed in the water as recorded in Matthew 3:16 which says:

> ***As soon as Jesus was baptized**, he **went up out of the water**. At that moment heaven was opened, and he saw the Spirit of God descending like a dove and alighting on him.*

The phrase "went up out of the water" means that when Jesus was baptized, He was soaked in the water. If the Lord Jesus was baptized by being sprinkled with water, He would be on a dry place since not much water is needed.

Likewise happened to the eunuch from Ethiopia as we read in Acts 8:36-38,

36 As they traveled along the road, they ***came to some water*** *and the eunuch said, "Look,* ***here is water****. What can stand in the way of my being baptized?" [37] 38 And he gave orders to stop the chariot.* ***Then both Philip and the eunuch went down into the water*** *and Philip baptized him.*

This shows that the eunuch was baptized by immersion. Now, if he was baptized by being sprinkled with water, they would not need to find a place with much water since they definitely would have brought along some water to drink on their journeys.

John 3:23 also states that where John the Baptist baptized people was a place with much water:

Now John also was baptizing at Aenon near Salim, because there was ***plenty of water****, and people were coming and* ***being baptized****.*

Died and Raised Up

Immersion baptism symbolizes to die or to be buried with Christ and to be raised up from the dead like Christ, as recorded in Romans 6:4:

We were therefore ***buried with him through baptism into death*** *in order that,* ***just as Christ was raised from the dead*** *through the glory of the Father,* ***we too may live a new life****.*

That is why in the process of baptism by immersion, those who are baptized will be immersed until the whole body is covered with water, which *symbolizes death (being buried)*, and then be helped to stand up again, *symbolizing the raising up into a new life*.

Indeed, some pastors or ministers of God assume that baptism is just a pro forma. But even if it is a kind of pro forma, the writer still wants to do what agrees with his conviction because obviously *to be baptized is part of the Great Commission of the Lord Jesus, so it ought to be carried out correctly*. The writer himself was baptized by immersion, but some of his children and in-laws were baptized by being sprinkled. However, the writer had asked some other pastor to baptize them again by immersion.

Abba, Father

Further, in Romans 8:15 we read:

> *The Spirit you received does not make you slaves, so that you live in fear again; rather, the Spirit you received brought about your* ***adoption to sonship****. And by him we cry, "****Abba, Father****."*

The verse above clearly says that at the very moment we accept Christ as our Lord and Savior, *we are saved*, and God gives us the Spirit of sonship *to become children of God, and by that Spirit we cry, "Abba, Father."*

The Meaning of Abba in Aramaic

The word *Abba* is originally Aramaic, the language spoken by Jesus Himself and often used in ancient Christian community. *Abba* is customary for children to call their father, like the term "Papa" today. The word *Abba* is uttered by the Lord Jesus and the Apostle Paul as an intimate term to depict their personal relationship with God. Thus, using the term *Abba, Father* for God expresses our true relationship with God. As Christians we often refer to God as Father; however only as a plain "word," not succeeded by respect nor obedience, while actually *Abba* should be applied with reverence to God.

Moreover, we often underestimate the term "Father" which was mentioned only once by the Lord Jesus (Mark 14:36) and twice by the Apostle Paul (Romans 8:15 and Galatians 4:6) in the New Testament. But as Jesus uttered this, we can feel the intensity of His intimate relationship with His Father.

In our new status as children of God, we obtain special rights and responsibilities or obligations attached to it. Therefore, we need to learn the rights and responsibilities or obligations of a child of God, and we will start first with the rights.

The Rights of God's Children

Many Christians are indifferent to their Christian life. This happens because they do not know the exceptional rights that God has bestowed upon them as His children. Therefore, let us study these prominent rights that we obtain as children of God.

1. Receive the Holy Spirit

Now it is God who makes both us and you stand firm in Christ. He anointed us.

(2 CORINTHIANS 1:21)

...set his seal of ownership on us, and put his Spirit in our hearts as a deposit, guaranteeing what is to come.

(2 CORINTHIANS 1:22)

Hence, at the very moment we receive Jesus Christ as our Lord and Savior, we also receive the Spirit of God (the Holy Spirit) in our hearts, and He will lead our lives as recorded in Romans 8:14:

For those who are led by the Spirit of God are the children of God.

So, all the children of God are to be led by the Spirit of God. Below are some guidance and help given by the Spirit of God to the children of God:

*In the same way, **the Spirit helps us in our weakness. We do not know what we ought to pray for**, but **the Spirit himself intercedes for us** through wordless groans.*

(ROMANS 8:26)

When we accept Christ as our Lord and Savior, we cannot pray, but the Holy Spirit will help us how we should pray, and even He himself will pray for us to God the Father.

...these are the things ***God has revealed to us by his Spirit****. The Spirit searches all things, even the deep things of God.*

(1 CORINTHIANS 2:10)

When we become children of God, God wants us to know Him personally. Therefore, God gives us His Spirit, the Holy Spirit, who will reveal to us even the deep or hidden things about God so that we can know God.

But you will ***receive power*** *when the Holy Spirit comes on you; and you will be my witnesses in Jerusalem, and in all Judea and Samaria, and to the ends of the earth.*

(ACTS 1:8)

The above verse explains that the Holy Spirit will give us power. What power? *First, the power to reject sins.* So, it is not true what some people think that since they have just repented or their faith is still weak, they have no power to reject sins.

To the church in Rome, the Apostle Paul explained in Romans chapter six that at the very moment we are saved, our old selves are crucified so that the body of sin might be destroyed, and we will be raised with a new body to bear the fruit of the Spirit to lead us to a holy life:

Rome 6:1 What shall we say, then? Shall we go on sinning so that grace may increase?

2 By no means! We are those who have died to sin; how can we live in it any longer?

3 Or don't you know that all of us who were baptized into Christ Jesus were baptized into his death?

4 We were therefore buried with him through baptism into death in order that, just as Christ was raised from the dead through the glory of the Father, we too may live a new life.

5 For if we have been united with him in a death like his, we will certainly also be united with him in a resurrection like his.

6 For we know that our old self was crucified with him so that the body ruled by sin might be done away with, that we should no longer be slaves to sin—

7 because anyone who has died has been set free from sin.

8 Now if we died with Christ, we believe that we will also live with him.

9 For we know that since Christ was raised from the dead, he cannot die again; death no longer has mastery over him.

10 The death he died, he died to sin once for all; but the life he lives, he lives to God.

11 In the same way, count yourselves dead to sin but alive to God in Christ Jesus.

12 Therefore do not let sin reign in your mortal body so that you obey its evil desires.

13 Do not offer any part of yourself to sin as an instrument of wickedness, but rather offer yourselves to God as those who have been brought from death to life; and offer every part of yourself to him as an instrument of righteousness.

14 For sin shall no longer be your master, because you are not under the law, but under grace.

15 What then? Shall we sin because we are not under the law but under grace? By no means!

16 Don't you know that when you offer yourselves to someone as obedient slaves, you are slaves of the one you obey—whether you are slaves to sin, which leads to death, or to obedience, which leads to righteousness?

17 But thanks be to God that, though you used to be slaves to sin, you have come to obey from your heart the pattern of teaching that has now claimed your allegiance.

18 You have been set free from sin and have become slaves to righteousness.

19 I am using an example from everyday life because of your human limitations. Just as you used to offer yourselves as slaves to impurity and to ever-increasing wickedness, so now offer yourselves as slaves to righteousness leading to holiness.

20 When you were slaves to sin, you were free from the control of righteousness.

21 What benefit did you reap at that time from the things you are now ashamed of? Those things result in death!

22 But now that you have been set free from sin and have become slaves of God, the benefit you reap leads to holiness, and the result is eternal life.

23 For the wages of sin is death, but the gift of God is eternal life in Christ Jesus our Lord.

Besides that, we are also given the power to cast away sickness, evil spirits, and even demons in the name of the Lord Jesus and the power to ask blessings for our families and for others as well.

For the Spirit God gave us ***does not make us timid****, but gives us* ***power****,* ***love*** *and* ***self-discipline****.*

(2 TIMOTHY 1:7)

Hence the Holy Spirit will give us strength and enable us to have love and to live orderly.

But the Advocate, the Holy Spirit, whom the Father will send in my name, will ***teach*** *you all things and will* ***remind you of everything I have said to you****.*

(JOHN 14:26)

One of the titles of the Holy Spirit is *paraklete*, an English word in Christian theology transliterated from the Greek noun *parakletos*, which means encourager, advisor (intercessor), helper, or comforter. Therefore, if we are sensitive and willing to follow the voice of the

Holy Spirit in our hearts, He will control our lives, teach us, remind us, and encourage us to be doers of the Word of God.

> *And I will ask the Father, and he will give you another advocate* ***to help you and be with you forever****.*
>
> *(JOHN 14:16)*

The Holy Spirit will be with us forever. Therefore, we need not be afraid to walk this life, even to face the tribulation or period of persecutions during the end times, for we will be accompanied perpetually by the very Person who is ready to help, comfort, advise, and give us strength.

2. We May Call God as Father

> *Because you are his sons, God sent the Spirit of his Son into our hearts, the Spirit who calls out, "****Abba, Father****."*
>
> *(GALATIANS 4:6)*

The writer knew a certain family with some children, and one of their children *is considered a child* by a government official. The family was very proud and happy. Yet we are not considered, instead we are acknowledged by God the Creator of heaven and earth, King of kings, as His own children.

When we observe or study any histories of the religions existing until now, there has been no single religion where the exalted or adored supreme personality, divinity, or god of it allows their adherents to call Him Father. No, none! Even if we study the Israelites as

God's chosen people, God did not allow nor give them the right to call Him Father. Exodus 20:7 says:

> *Thou shalt not take the name of the* LORD *thy God in vain; for the* LORD *will not hold him guiltless that taketh his name in vain.*
>
> (KJV)

This verse does not only forbid to call God as Father, but even mentioning the name of the LORD* carelessly would be considered guilty. That is why unto this day, the nation of Israel never dared to mention the name of the LORD. For example, when there is a verse in the Torah mentioning the name of the LORD, the Israelites would replace the word LORD in that verse with the word "Adonai," which means Master or my Lord as they read the verse since they fear lest they mention the name of the LORD incorrectly either in their speech, situations, attitudes, positions, or others, so that they would be considered careless and found guilty.

*In the Bible produced by LAI (Indonesian Bible Society), "TUHAN" ("LORD") is used for God's name, all capitalized, as the translation of the word "YHWH" or in Hebrew "יהוה." pronounced as Yahweh or Jehovah, while "Tuhan" as the translation of the word "אֱלֹהִים" ("Elohim") is His designation.

In the New Testament too, the verse is reconfirmed in the Lord's Prayer. In this prayer (Matthew 6:9), the Lord Jesus started like this:

> *Our Father in heaven,* ***hallowed be your name****...*

Now the meaning of the phrase "hallowed be your name" bears the conception that the name of God, namely, "LORD," ought to be treated holy. The name of God must not be carelessly or inappropriately mentioned as if it is just any simple or common word or name which seems cheap and unworthy that might be mentioned and treated heedlessly as we please.

Then in Matthew 12:36 Jesus said:

But I tell you that men ***will have to give account*** *on the day of judgment* ***for every careless word*** *they have spoken.*

So, if we carelessly utter a word, not only the word "LORD" but any other word as well, we will have to give account for it later at the Day of Judgment. For more details, please read the writer's book entitled *Our Speech*.

3. We Are Allowed to Enter into Heaven

Some people might already know that the writer has been given the opportunity to learn for twenty years the five religions known existing. The writer has been attending church since his childhood and was baptized as a teenager. In 1980, the writer's first college year, there was a subject about comparison of religions. In the course of studying this subject, the writer realized that there were four other different main religions and Christianity was not the only one: Roman Catholic, Hinduism, Buddhism, and Moslem. The writer longed to learn them all and find out which is the right and true one. When the writer presented or conveyed about this matter, sometimes people asked him, "What did you discover during those times that you finally decided to choose Christianity?" To answer this question, the writer could explain extensively, adequately, or simply as time allowed.

When simply, the writer usually would start explaining what religion is. Now, religion involved at least two issues. *First, religion involves human relationship with God.* If the relationship is between a human being and his fellowmen, it is called social science, law issue, ethics, and so on. If the relationship is between human beings and the universe or the stars, it could be astronomy or astrology and so on. Religion is about the relationship between God and man. *Second, how to enter heaven,* because these five religions all believe that there is another life after death. And in this afterlife, some people would enter heaven and some would go to hell. Each religion has its own terms and ways to enter heaven or go to hell.

Then the writer would ask the inquirer, "Sir, you surely have a house, haven't you? Would you permit anybody to enter into your house and live there?" The answer would definitely be, "No!" "So, then who would be permitted?" "My wife, my children, and my family, of course."

Now, what is heaven? *Heaven is God's house.* Therefore, who is permitted to enter it? *Definitely, His children!*

Then the writer would ask them again, "If you see some children who are good, nice, and sweet, would you permit them to come into your house and live there?" The answer would be, "No, I wouldn't." Why would they not be granted the permission even though they are good, nice, and sweet? The answer surely would be, "Since *they are not our children.*" Hence, similarly people who have tried to be good, nice, and sweet would not be permitted to enter the Kingdom of Heaven because of *their status, as they are not God's children!*

In the Bible, it is clearly stated in 2 Corinthians 5:1:

Now we know that if the earthly tent we live in is destroyed, ***we have a building from God, an eternal house in heaven,*** *not built by human hands.*

Thus, this verse explains that later when our earthly tent or mortal body we live in is destroyed or when we die, God has already prepared a place in heaven for our spirit or our resurrected body to dwell in it.

Further, in John 14:2,3 we read:

My Father's house has many rooms; *if that were not so, would I have told you that I am going there to prepare a place for you?*

(JOHN 14:2)

Since we are His children, God as the Owner of Heaven has already prepared a place for each of us.

And it continued in verse 3 which says:

And if I go and prepare a place for you, ***I will come back and take you to be with me*** *that you also may be where I am.*

(JOHN 14:3)

It is explained here that someday in the future, the Lord Jesus would come for us, either in His second coming or at the moment we leave this life. That is why when a Christian passed away, it is commonly said that he or she "has gone to Heavenly home," for we as Christians leave this world to go to a place called home which God has already prepared for us in Heaven.

4. God's Promise to Provide for Us in This World

In 1 Peter 1:3–5, it is explained:

> *Praise be to the God and Father of our Lord Jesus Christ! In his great mercy he has given us new birth into a living hope through the resurrection of Jesus Christ from the dead.*
>
> (1 PETER 1:3)

> *...and into an inheritance that can never perish, spoil or fade—kept in heaven* ***for you.***
>
> (1 PETER 1:4)

Thus, verses 3–4 explain about our process of being saved through Jesus Christ and that later when we die, there would already be a place reserved for us in heaven.

However, in verse 5 it is said:

> *...who through faith* ***are shielded by God's power*** *until the coming of the salvation that is ready to be revealed in the last time.*
>
> (1 PETER 1:5)

This verse is the continuation of verse 4, after the phrase "kept in heaven for *you*." And who is meant by "you" here? *You* in this verse are people including us who have accepted Christ as Lord and Savior, as explained previously in verses 3–4. Hence there is already a place prepared for us in heaven. Even though we have the promise of a place assured for us in heaven, at present we are still living in this world and awaiting that life in heaven which we would be able to enjoy only after we leave this world or die. This is explained by the phrase "until the coming of salvation." However, as children of God, we are shielded by God's power, and He will take care of us and provide for us in this world by His strength.

For more details, please read again the writer's book entitled *God's Promise to Provide*.

5. Becoming the Object of God's Love

Romans 8:30–32 explains:

*30 And those he predestined, he also called; those he called, he also justified; those he justified, **he also glorified**.*

31 What, then, shall we say in response to these things? If God is for us, who can be against us?

*32 He **who did not spare his own Son**, but gave him up for us all—**how will he not also**, along with him, **graciously give us all things**?*

These verses explain that God willingly sacrificed His own Son to save us sinners. So then, would He not do other things which are much simpler for us, His redeemed children? Yet, God's desire is not only to give us all things, but even more than that—*God really wants to glorify us*.

Today there are pastors who say that after we have been redeemed through the sacrifice of Christ Jesus, we must serve Him as a token of our gratefulness. It is certainly not wrong to serve, but if we think we are redeemed so as to become servants of God, we might hurt

God's heart. Such a concept indicates that we think God redeems us not because He loves us, but so that God can have many servants. The truth is, God redeems us to become His children, not to become His servants since God has a host of angels as His servants and *that we would become the object of God's love*. The writer believes that when we get married, we long to have children. When we finally get children, we have no plans at all to make our children as our servants, rather to make them the object of our love. If our goal concerning our children were to make them as our servants, we would send them to school only until they finished elementary school. We need not send them to a higher level of education nor provide special facilities and all kinds of comforts. For more details, please read again the writer's book entitled *To Be Children of God or Servants of God.*

6. Helping Us in Our Difficulties

God understands that when we accept Christ as Lord and Savior, we are still to dwell in this world for some time and do not go directly to heaven. God promises that He will take care of us. Yet He also understands that as long as we live our temporary life in this world, there will be many problems and difficulties we must face. Therefore, in Matthew 11:28 the Lord Jesus clearly said:

> ***Come*** *to me, all you who are weary and burdened, and I will give you rest.*

God really wants to help us, so He uses the word *come*. He wants us to immediately approach Him and come to Him when we face difficulties because He wants to help us solve all our problems right away so that we can be released or freed from them.

When this topic is being discussed, there are often some who wondered, "Though I have been praying for my problems and made every effort I could, still help doesn't seem to come." Perhaps one of the answers is related to this verse in Mark 11:24:

> *Therefore I tell you, whatever you ask for in prayer,* ***believe that you have received it****, and it will be yours.*

So, one of the keys to our prayer being answered is *to believe that we have received it*. This means that if we ask God for something, we should believe that He has already prepared it for us, and then we just wait to receive it and do not go to any other personality to appeal for it since our request has been granted by God. From the writer's experience concerning this verse, in some instances, the problems were still unanswered, no resolution from God. As the writer reflected upon this case, he found out that it happened because he kept an ambiguous attitude at that time. Yes, he asked for God's help, but on the other hand, he exerted himself to overcome the problems by his own strength or sought help from other sources. It could be seeking help from officials, acquaintances, or anybody. Some other people may be seeking help from some "smart people/wise men" or from other gods. This attitude shows that we don't believe God has granted our request.

7. God Wants to Be Close to Us

> ***Come near to God and he will come near to you.*** *Wash your hands, you sinners, and purify your hearts, you double-minded.*
>
> *(James 4:8)*

When we study this verse, "Come near to God and he will come near to you," we will see clearly that the initiative of drawing near or approaching must begin with us: when we draw near to God, then He will voluntarily draw near to us. But there are necessarily some conditions. First, *cleanse your hands*. This means that we have to cast away our sins to ask for God's forgiveness. Therefore, let us begin our prayers with asking God's forgiveness for all our sins and wrongdoings, along with a serious intention to relinquish any sin.

Then "purify your hearts, ye double minded," which actually means that we must keep our hearts clean and not be double-minded or ambiguous. We must trust God completely.

The writer pondered on how "Come near to God and he will come near to you" can be clearly perceptible. During one of his recent vacations, the writer just got the meaning, and this might be the true one. At that very time, the writer and his family were faring on a cruiser and we have bought an Internet package provided by the ship. This cruiser harbored at several ports, and we could go ashore to enjoy the beauty of the cities. Once when we went ashore, his wife received several news via WhatsApp she had to answer. The communication through WhatsApp seemed to run well. Yet quite soon she found out that her messages failed and were not sent. She was quite in panic because the news she conveyed were important. After talking with our children, we then realized that our position was too far from the ship; thus we could not make use of the Internet signal since the provider was on board. Consequently, we went back closer to the ship to obtain the active signal. Likewise, we must draw closer to God so that we can have an active line to communicate with Him. How can we draw closer to God? By *setting aside a special quiet time daily to have an intensive fellowship with God*: reading the Bible, praising God, and praying.

When we draw closer to the Father, He will bless us and shape us to become His children who would please Him.

> *Who may ascend the mountain of the Lord?* ***Who may stand in his holy place****?*
>
> *(PSALM 24:3)*
>
> *4 The one who has* ***clean hands*** *and a* ***pure heart****, who* ***does not trust in an idol*** *or* ***swear by a false god****.*
>
> *5 They will* ***receive blessing from the Lord*** *and* ***vindication from God their Savior****.*
>
> *6 Such is the generation of those* ***who seek him****,* ***who seek your face****, God of Jacob.*

Those are the seven rights we are endowed with as God's children. Now we will continue to the second main topic, the responsibilities of God's children.

The Responsibilities of God's Children

The rights owned by God's children are settled for us to receive. However, the responsibilities or obligations of God's children *must* be carried out as a logical consequence in our status or position as God's children.

There are two prominent responsibilities of God's children:

1. To Maintain the Status as God's Children

*We have come to share in Christ, **if indeed we hold our original conviction firmly to the very end.***

(HEBREWS 3:14)

All these rights specifically related to salvation, to enter the Kingdom of Heaven, and so on will be our privilege if we maintain our status as children of God unto the end of our lives. If we let loose this status, it clearly would make us no more as children of God. We cannot enter the Kingdom of Heaven, cannot enter the Father's House.

The Apostle Paul also mentioned this issue in 2 Timothy 4:7:

*I have fought the good fight, I have finished the race, **I have kept the faith**.*

There is a very important phrase, "I have kept the faith." So, it is not just finishing the course or the race till the finish line, but also keeping our faith until the end.

There are at least two things causing a child of God to lose his or her status as God's child:

First: Intentionally or Consciously Cast Loose Their Status

*No one can serve two masters. Either you will hate the one and love the other, or you will be devoted to the one and despise the other. **You cannot serve both God and money**.*

(MATTHEW 6:24 NIV)

or

> *No man can serve two masters: for either he will hate the one, and love the other; or else he will hold to the one, and despise the other.* ***Ye cannot serve God and mammon.***
>
> (Matthew 6:24 KJV)

We often read about some people who give up his religious beliefs to gain certain projects, positions, and facilities or to marry somebody.

As it was mentioned earlier, the reason someone easily abandon or cast loose his or her status as a child of God is that the person does not know nor understand how valuable the rights he or she receives as God's child.

Explaining about the Kingdom of Heaven, the Lord Jesus used a parable to describe the preciousness of one's salvation. So, if the person knew this, which was likened to a hidden treasure, he/she would be willing to sell all of his/her possessions to obtain the treasure.

> *The kingdom of heaven is like treasure hidden in a field. When a man found it, he hid it again, and then in his joy went and sold all he had and bought that field.*
>
> *(Matthew 13:44)*

The Apostle Paul even counted everything in the world but dung, as thrash, compared with the rights he got through Jesus Christ.

> *What is more, I consider everything a loss because of the surpassing worth of knowing Christ Jesus my Lord, for whose sake I have lost all things. I consider them garbage, that I may gain Christ.*
>
> *(Philippians 3:8)*

***Second*: Cast Loose by Deception**

> *For **false messiahs** and **false prophets** will appear and perform great signs and wonders **to deceive, if possible, even the elect**.*
>
> (*MATTHEW 24:24*)

Nowadays, in the end times, many false messiahs and false prophets will appear. Therefore, we really must have adequate knowledge of the Word of God so that we will not be fooled easily. For more explanation, please read again the writer's book entitled *Heaviest Temptations*.

2. The Behavior of God's Children

When we decide to accept Christ as our Lord and Savior, we will be saved and granted the status as God's children. And as God's children, we are required to behave as such, according to Romans 8:29:

> *For those God foreknew he also predestined to be conformed to **the image of his Son**, that he might be the firstborn among many brothers and sisters.*

A Christian's spiritual growth is proportional to his or her likeness of Jesus Christ. To be like Christ is not something we can work out by ourselves, rather it is God's work that will shape us through His Holy Spirit in us, as recorded in Philippians 2:12–13;

> *12 Therefore, my dear friends, as you have always obeyed—not only in my presence, but now much more in my*

*absence—**continue to work out your salvation with fear and trembling**.*

*13 for **it is God who works in you to will and to act in order to fulfill his good purpose**.*

These verses explain that God will shape us, but we must do our duty or take our responsibility, that is, to "work out your salvation with fear and trembling." What is actually to work out our own salvation? The essence is to keep holding on to our faith till the end, striving to strengthen it by way of the following:

First, routinely spend a devotional quiet time, read the Bible diligently, meditate upon the Word of God, and *do it in our lives*. Then learn to thank and praise God either in good or in bad conditions, and set aside ample time to pray regularly.

Second, diligently attend worship services, and do not skip worshiping in the church.

Third, have a regular family worship at home.

To behave appropriately as a child of God is obligatory as a logical consequence of that status along with the rights we receive accordingly.

We often read about common people who were married to some members of the Royal family. So, they eventually belonged to the Royal family and their statuses were raised up. They might often be reprimanded for their improper attire, such as sleeveless gowns; be criticized for their skirts, either too short or too tight, even for the colors which were considered too loud or not elegant; and so on. Initially, some of them were indifferent and didn't really care much, but later on they relented and agreed to fit in. Why would they finally obey? Of course, it is a logical consequence of the new status they received. So, if they agree to become members of the Royal family, they not only would get the proper rights, but they would also have responsibilities and obligations accordingly.

> *Seek the Lord while he may be found; call on him while he is near.*
>
> *(ISAIAH 55:6)*

THE FOUNDATIONS OF CHRISTIANITY

Yunus Ciptawilangga, MBA

The Foundations of Christianity

Human race are social beings. Normally, as social beings, we would interact with our fellowmen. Yet, we are God's created beings as well. As created beings, we certainly have a relationship with the Creator. In Christian faith, man was created in the image or likeness of God (Gen.1:26–27). Consequently, in their relationship with the unseen Creator (John 1:18 and Hebrew 11:6), humans often use methods or models of interactions similar to those practiced in their daily life, for example, by prioritizing and building trust, spending time together, and developing an atmosphere of love, respect, and more.

Comparing Each Other's Faith

Consciously or not, we sometimes tend to compare our conditions or our children with others', for example, concerning their physical developments. *See, my child can walk at this age, while other children have not learned yet.* When our child has entered school, we also tend to compare his or her physical developments with other children, to know who is taller and sometimes to appraise who is more handsome or pretty. We also like to compare our child's intelligence with other children's, and so on. Obviously, we not only tend to compare our child and our family members with others, but to compare ourselves too with others.

Even in church we oftentimes tend to compare our faith with others'. When we see our friends being active in the church ministries, we assume that their faith is more mature. When we hear a member of the church singing with a beautiful voice as a soloist in front of the congregation, we are of the opinion that the person is not only a man or woman of faith, but also one gifted by God with a special talent. If we meet a Sunday school teacher, we say in our hearts, *Oh, he or she must be a person with a great faith.* We also respect or honor people who diligently spread the Gospel, driven by their admirable faith. And if we hear someone preaching well, we consider the person's faith excellent. Moreover, if he or she can preach in front of a big congregation or audience, his or her faith must be very inspiring.

Our evaluations or judgments described above, assuming that others are better based merely on our eyesight or our hearings, are not entirely false. The author would like to make this comparison: the condition regarding the outward appearances could be likened to a building. By this the author means a building might look good or not good and grand or simple, but all are just external, only from the outside. However, there is another more important matter that needs a special attention, namely, the foundation of the building. Likewise, when we talk about faith, there is a most important matter that must be highlighted, and that is the foundation of our faith. Why is the foundation of a building or of our faith so important? It is because the foundation actually sustains the building. If the base or the foundation of a building is not firm, then the building can collapse easily. So too with faith. Occasionally we heard of some activists who were amazingly diligent in serving the Lord and had become "God's instruments" but suddenly receded and disappeared. They were not active anymore, and even some left their faith for another belief. How could this happen?

The Foundations of Faith

When we notice, the cases discussed above are, in fact, the results of the fragility or lack of strength concerning the foundations of faith. The activities might look good, yet the foundations of faith were not strong. Therefore, the foundations of faith are very important and fundamental for us to comprehend and possess. Indeed, there are many important and fundamental things in the Christian faith, but the author will discuss only what are considered most important.

First Foundation: Jesus Is the Messiah

This is recorded among others in Matthew 16:13–20:

> *16:13 When Jesus came to the region of Caesarea Philippi, he asked his disciples, "Who do people say the Son of Man is?"*

14 They replied, "Some say John the Baptist; others say Elijah; and still others, Jeremiah or one of the prophets."

15 "But what about you?" he asked. "Who do you say I am?"

16 Simon Peter answered, "You are the Messiah, the Son of the living God."

17 Jesus replied, "Blessed are you, Simon son of Jonah, for this was not revealed to you by flesh and blood, but by my Father in heaven.

18 And I tell you that you are Peter, and on this rock I will build my church, and the gates of Hades will not overcome it.

19 I will give you the keys of the kingdom of heaven; whatever you bind on earth will be bound in heaven, and whatever you loose on earth will be loosed in heaven."

20 Then he ordered his disciples not to tell anyone that he was the Messiah.

From the verses above, some said that the foundation of the Christian faith is Peter since in verses 18–19 it is written: "And I tell you that you are *Peter*, and *on this rock I will build my church*, and the gates of Hades will not overcome it.

19 I will give you *the keys of the kingdom of heaven*; whatever you bind on earth will be bound in heaven, and whatever you loose on earth will be loosed in heaven."

Is it possible that the foundation of the Christian faith or the foundation of the church is planted on some man or on a human being? No, it is definitely impossible, for in Jeremiah 17:5, it is said:

> *This what the Lord says:* ***Cursed is the one who trusts in man****, who depends on flesh for his strength and whose heart turns away from the LORD.*

So if the church is founded on man, it is certainly contradictory to this verse. Beyond that, the Bible records that Peter was one of Jesus' disciples who denied Him three times. (See Matthew 26:30–35, 69–75.) Even afterward, subsequent to the events, Paul once reprimanded Peter because he saw that Peter's behavior was hypocritical and not in accordance with the truth of the Gospel. (See Galatians 2:11–14.) Therefore, neither the Christian faith nor the church can be founded on Peter who was a mere human being.

Using a Name as a Symbol

> *And I tell you that you are* ***Peter****, and* ***on this rock I will build my church****.*

"Peter" is a word which means "rock," and indeed God often called people with a name that symbolized something, such as in Hosea 1:6:

> *Gomer conceived again and gave birth to a daughter. Then the Lord said to Hosea, "Call her Lo-Ruhamah (which means*

'not loved'), for I will no longer show love to Israel, should at all forgive them."

Obviously the name Lo-Ruhamah is *a symbol* that God would no more have mercy upon the house of Israel and would utterly take them away. In other words, God would no longer show love to the house of Israel and would not forgive them. Also in Hosea 1:9, it is stated:

Then the Lord said, "Call him Lo-Ammi (which means 'not my people'), for you are not my people, and I am not your God."

Hence, what are the foundations of the Christian faith?

One most important foundation of the Christian faith is recorded in Matthew 16:16.

In verse 15 *Jesus asked, "Who do you say I am?"*

*Simon Peter answered, "You are **the Messiah**, the Son of the living God"*

(*VERSE 16).*

This is again emphasized in verse 20:

*Then he ordered his disciples not to tell anyone that **he was the Messiah**.*

So it is clear that one most important foundation of the Christian faith is the conviction or the belief that Jesus is Christ, the Messiah. That is the foundation of the church, and that is the foundation of the Christian faith.

The Work of the Father in Peter

Regardless of Peter's weaknesses, Jesus honored the work of the Father in Peter (verse 17). *Jesus said:*

> *Jesus replied, "Blessed are you, Simon son of Jonah,* ***for this was not revealed to you by flesh and blood, but by my Father in heaven.****"*

Amidst the teachings of the Pharisees and Sadducees, and the confusion among the crowds as well, Peter declared something right even though his statement that Jesus was the Messiah did not truly come out of his own mind but from God the Father through him. The foundation of the Christian faith is definitely not Peter, yet his confession that Jesus was the Messiah is followed with some explanation in verse 19:

> *I will give you the keys of the kingdom of heaven; whatever you bind on earth will be bound in heaven, and whatever you loose on earth will be loosed in heaven.*

At a glance, the verse above describes that Jesus gave Peter the keys of the Kingdom of Heaven:

> *I will give you the keys of the kingdom of heaven...*

But when we read further:

> *...whatever you bind on earth will be bound in heaven, and whatever you loose on earth will be loosed in heaven.*

This part explains that there is a connection between what is done in the world and what will happen in heaven. Thus from the verse we are given the understanding of whether at the end we are to enter into the Kingdom of Heaven or not, which would be determined by what we do in this world. This means that if *during our lives in the world* we confess Jesus is the Messiah, we will enter heaven, but if we never made this confession, we will not enter heaven. This also means that if someone dies and has never confessed Jesus is the Messiah during his or her life, there will be no way for that person to enter into the Kingdom of Heaven. So, if the foundation of Christian faith is Peter, the opportunity to enter the Kingdom of Heaven would end when Peter died, which also means the end of Christianity. Meanwhile, in the verse after Peter's confession, the Lord Jesus declared that the foundation of the Christian faith is eternal:

> *And I tell you that you are Peter, and on this rock I will build my church, and* ***the gates of Hades will not overcome it****.*
>
> (MATTHEW 16:18)

Therefore the paragraph of Matthew 16:13–20 might be simplified as follows:

> *16:13 When Jesus came to the region of Caesarea Philippi, he asked his disciples, "Who do people say the Son of Man is?"*
>
> *14 They replied, "Some say John the Baptist; others say Elijah; and still others, Jeremiah or one of the prophets."*
>
> *15 "But what about you?" he asked. "Who do you say I am?"*

16 Simon Peter answered, "You are the Messiah, the Son of the living God."

17 Jesus replied, "Blessed are you, Simon son of Jonah, for this was not revealed to you by flesh and blood, but by my Father in heaven.

18 And I tell you that you are Peter, and on ***this confession that Jesus is the Messiah*** *(this rock) I will build my church, and the gates of Hades will not overcome it.*

19 I will give to ***anyone who confesses that Jesus is the Messiah*** *(you) the keys of the kingdom of heaven; whatever you bind on earth will be bound in heaven, and whatever you loose on earth will be loosed in heaven."*

20 Then he ordered his disciples not to tell anyone that he was the Messiah.

The Meaning of the Word "Messiah"

Messiah is Christ. The two words are of the same meaning, whereas Messiah is in Hebrew and Christ (Christos) in Greek. Messiah or Christ is a title, which means *The Anointed One*. This title is given to *The Savior* (or *The Deliverer* or *The Redeemer*) whose coming had been prophesied by the prophets and was fulfilled by the birth of the Lord Jesus, as recorded among others in Luke 2:11 as follows:

Today in the town of David a Savior has been born to you; he is the Messiah, the Lord. (NIV)

For unto you is born this day in the city of David a Saviour, which is Christ the Lord. (KJV)

Jesus Is the Savior and the Lord

Luke 2:11 above said:

Today in the town of David ***a Savior*** *has been born to you; he is the Messiah,* ***the Lord.***

(NIV)

For unto you is born this day in the city of David ***a Saviour,*** *which is* ***Christ the Lord.***

(KJV)

Here we can draw at least two meanings:

First, *Jesus Christ is the Savior*. Second, *Jesus Christ is the Lord*.

Jesus Christ Is the Savior

In John 14:6 it is written:

> *Jesus answered, "**I am the way and the truth and the life**. No one comes to the Father except through me."*

The Christian faith is based on one conviction that *salvation is made possible only through Jesus Christ*. This is confirmed in Acts 4:12:

> ***Salvation is found in no one else**, for there is no other name under heaven given to mankind by which we must be saved.*

Evidently, we are given this most important knowledge that the only way to eternal salvation is only through *Jesus Christ, the Savior*.

Thus Christian faith is based on the belief that man cannot pay for his or her sins and cannot get away from the penalty of those sins, except that he or she acknowledges individually as a sinful human being and accept Jesus Christ as his or her personal Savior because Jesus Christ had died on the cross to bear the sins of mankind.

Jesus Christ Is the Lord

If we truly believe that Jesus Christ is the Lord, we would never have any doubt about His resurrection, for He is the Lord. As it is clear in Mark 16:6:

> *"Don't be alarmed," he said. "You are looking for Jesus the Nazarene, who was crucified. **He has risen**! He is not here. See the place where they laid him."*

We would not question or argue about the truth of the verse which mentions that Jesus has risen from the death if we believe He is the Lord or that Jesus was taken up to heaven as is recorded among others in Acts 1:9:

After he said this, ***he was taken up*** *before their very eyes, and a cloud hid him from their sight.*

Indeed, we would never question this nor doubt about this. Therefore, anyone who confesses to be a Christian yet still doubt about the resurrection of Jesus the Lord or about His ascension is actually not in doubt of His resurrection, rather he or she does not believe that Jesus Christ is the Lord.

If we truly believe that Jesus Christ is the Lord, we would be in line with what is said in Proverbs 3:5:

Trust in the Lord with all your heart and lean not on your own understanding...

Hence, we surely would believe in Jesus Christ with all our hearts because we are convinced that Jesus Christ is the Lord and put our trust wholeheartedly in Him. And we would not rely on man, for even if he is considered very great, he could never exceed the Lord. Nor would we rely on our own strength since our strength is unreliable and inadequate. And we definitely would always long to be close to the Lord because we believe that *Jesus Christ is the Lord.*

Faith and Prayer

And we would be blessed because we trust in the Lord and put our hope in Him, as recorded in Jeremiah 17:7:

But blessed is the one who trusts in the Lord, whose confidence is in him.

Hence, if we truly believe that Jesus Christ is the Lord, we would faithfully and diligently worship Him. We would always strive to be near Him and would always pray surrendering all our plans to Him.

And if we believe that Jesus Christ is the Lord, we would long to be baptized as we can read in Romans 10:9:

If you declare with your mouth, "Jesus is Lord," and believe in your heart that God raised him from the dead, you will be saved.

And in Matthew 28:19–20:

19 Therefore go and make disciples of all nations, baptizing them in the name of the Father and of the Son and of the Holy Spirit,

20 and teaching them to obey everything I have commanded you. And surely I am with you always, to the very end of the age.

Consciously and Understandingly

Romans 10:9 contains at least two significant things. The first is "If you *declare* with your mouth, 'Jesus is Lord.'"

The word "declare" here bears the meaning of "being conscious" or "consciously" while uttering something. So, it is clear that declaring is done consciously or with awareness, for only by being conscious of our condition can we confess something sincerely and rightly.

The second is "and *believe* in your heart that God raised him from the dead, you will be saved."

The word "believe" here implies that we "understand" because we cannot believe in something we do not understand. Even though we may not understand entirely, we have at least some understanding of the matter, like the author's grandson who one day asked, "Grandpa, of the moon and the sun, which one is bigger?" The author answered, "The sun." The boy replied, "Why then does it seem so small?" The author took a book and held it upward. Then he moved backward and further backward. "You see the book looks smaller, doesn't it?" "Yes, it looks smaller," the boy responded. "The sun looks small because it is far away from us," explained the author to his grandson. Although the boy did not understand completely, at least he got some understanding at that moment which led him to believe.

Why is this necessary to be conveyed? Because as Christians, we need to introspect ourselves. This means that we have to examine our inner condition and recognize whether we in our lives have ever consciously and understandingly accepted Jesus Christ as our personal Lord and Savior. Yes, we could have been baptized or have made a confession of faith as teenagers, and even some of us were baptized as children or babies. When we were still small, we surely did not understand the significance of these all. Yet we should also flash back to ponder whether our confession of faith, when we as teenagers accepted Jesus Christ as Lord and Savior, was done consciously and understandingly. If it is not so, we probably have not accepted Jesus Christ as Lord and Savior yet. In that case, we need to accept Jesus Christ as Lord and Savior right now, consciously and understandingly.

Second Foundation: The Bible Is the Word of God

The second foundation of Christianity is the conviction or the belief that the Bible is the Word of God. The Bible was written in the span of more than 1600 years by forty different authors. Nevertheless the contents of all the books are not contradictory, rather complementary and explain each other. Some people asked the author why he can write Christian books since he has never studied in any theological school or seminary. Indeed, the author is given the ability to write by God's mercy. And habitually, whenever the author wants to understand a certain word or phrase, he just search the word in the Bible. Usually he is able to find quite a few verses that explain that word or that phrase.

And besides, the Bible describes various events in a coherent and credible fashion, beginning with the creation of the heavens and the earth, then the creation of man, and ending up on the threshold of eternity. Furthermore, archaeological discoveries support the integrity of its records, both historically and geographically. For example, the ruins of Queen of Sheba's palace site was recently discovered. The books of 1 Kings (10:1–13) and 2 Chronicles (9:1–12) explain that when Solomon became king of the Israelites, the Queen of Sheba came to visit him in Jerusalem.

And also in the tomb of Jonah the Prophet, there were recently found inscriptions which describe the city of Nineveh. Moreover, its accuracy and transcriptions for us were also reinforced by the scrolls found in the cave of Qumran, on the banks of the Dead Sea.

Many prophecies in the Bible were already fulfilled, for example, the prophecies regarding the coming of the Lord Jesus. There were hundreds of prophecies about the coming of the Messiah and forty major prophecies about the birth of the Lord Jesus fulfilled. But most important of all is that the whole Bible is true. Hence not just historically correct or accurate, but the content, namely, the verses, are truly correct. Since long in the past, the author has been the type of person who pays much attention to his family. That is why the author read a lot and attended seminars on family building and then tried to put the teachings into practice. But after experimenting on various theories, suggestions, and admonitions, the author finally realized that only what is written in the Bible is true and right.

Babies and Adults

So if we truly believe that the Bible is the Word of God, we certainly would be thirsty for the Word of God as described in 1 Peter 2:2:

Like newborn babies, crave pure spiritual milk, so that by it you may grow up in your salvation.

Why is it put here "like newborn babies?" Because when the baby's milk comes late, even a bit late while it is feeding time yet, the baby would immediately cry for it. So too should we be regarding the thirst for God's Word. When there is no desire in us to read and listen to God's Word, we must question our faith, then, for if we have a living and growing faith, we would be like a baby who will cry instantly when it is time to get its milk.

Then further in Hebrew 5:13–14, we read:

> *Anyone who lives on milk, being still an infant, is not acquainted with the teaching about righteousness. But solid food is for the mature, who by constant use have trained themselves to distinguish good from evil.*

So, if we are already Christians for quite long or quite some time, we surely cannot feed just on milk. If a child feeds on milk continually, he would look sweet, but if an adult continually feeds on milk, he would be laughed at. As we grow up, we naturally look for solid food. When we listen to God's Word or read it through, we do not look for just pleasant Words or nice messages, but we should be open-minded to rebukes and advices. So, when we hear the rebuking Words and feel offended or get angry, it signifies that we are still childish in our faith.

Thus, what should we do?

We should be like the early church described in Acts 17:11:

> *Now the Berean Jews were of more noble character than those in Thessalonica, for they received the message with great eagerness and examined the Scriptures every day to see if what Paul said was true.*

Hence, we should become God's children who are open-minded and enthusiastic while listening to God's Word, rather than listen reluctantly bothered by sleepiness. Then we also should make time each day to earnestly study God's Word or search the Scriptures, not just reading through.

Some might ask, "Sir, we have read the Bible several times from the book of Genesis to the book of Revelation. Actually, how many times do we have to read it?"

John 10:4–5 says:

*4 When he has brought out all his own, he goes on ahead of them, and his sheep follow him because **they know his voice**.*

*5 But they will never follow a stranger; in fact, they will run away from him **because they do not recognize a stranger's voice**.*

Now these verses explain that we as children of God must be able to recognize the voice of God our Father. Yet this is not enough; we have to be able to distinguish the voice of the shepherd from the voice of strangers. So, how many times do we have to read the Bible? Well, until we *can distinguish* between the Word of God and the false teachings. That is what the Lord requires from us. (Please read the author's book *The Characteristics of God's Children*.)

The Third Foundation: Doers of the Word

The third foundation of Christianity is explained among others in Luke 6:47–49:

47 As for everyone who comes to me and hears my words and puts them into practice, I will show you what they are like.

48 They are like a man building a house, who dug down deep and laid the foundation on rock. When a flood came, the torrent struck that house but could not shake it, because it was well built.

49 But the one who hears my words and does not put them into practice is like a man who built a house on the ground without a foundation. The moment the torrent struck that house, it collapsed and its destruction was complete.

The pericope above explains that hearing the Word of God and doing it, as one of the foundations of Christianity, would in fact be an effort to strengthen the Christian faith. So when there is bitterness, temptation, and even persecution, our faith would be unshakeable. But on the contrary, whenever we only hear and do not do the Word of God, then surely, we do not put our faith fully in the Lord Jesus; and when there are bitterness, temptation, and persecution, we would fall, even fall away.

If we read the history, on November 1, 1755, Lisbon, the capital of Portugal, was hit by a bad earthquake which reached to 8–9 on the Richter scale and a devastating tsunami, which destroyed eighty percent of the buildings in the city of Lisbon and the remaining twenty percent heavily damaged. And if we observe closely, from the buildings that were not destroyed, one was found relatively intact, the National Palace of Pena. All parts of that building were intact, with nothing changed even in the least, except the clock tower which had collapsed. Why can this building remain intact even now? Because it *was built on a granite rock hill*. Perhaps, this building depicts what the Lord Jesus said that when a house is built on a rock, even though the flood comes, the house will not collapse. Likewise, to become hearers and doers of the Word shows that we are people who build our Christian faith on Jesus Christ the Solid Rock as our foundation. On the contrary, eighty percent of the collapsed houses can be likened to the houses built without foundations.

Our Personal Experience with the Lord

Why can hearing and doing God's Word strengthen our faith? *Because our faith must be based on our personal experience with the Lord.*

This is similar to Job's experience:

> ***My ears had heard of*** *you but now* ***my eyes have seen you****.*
>
> *Therefore I despise myself and repent in dust and ashes.*
>
> (JOB 42:5–6)

So the Christian faith is insufficient when the foundation on which to build is *only by the hearing*; for example: *Oh I have heard the testimony of A; the Lord helped him*, or *I have heard the testimony of B; the Lord healed him*, or *I have heard the testimony of C; his problems were solved by God.* All these are not enough, though. We must have *our own experience with God.* We ourselves should feel the power of the Lord in our lives. We ourselves should feel the presence of the Lord in our lives because this personal experience with the Lord would become another strong foundation of our faith.

The same thing happened to the Samaritans, who said in John 4:42:

> *They said to the woman, "We no longer believe just because of what you said; now* ***we have heard for ourselves, and we know*** *that this man really is the Savior of the world."*

So the foundation of our faith must be based on our own experience with the Lord too, just like the Samaritans. They had heard the Lord Jesus themselves and saw Him themselves, as He stayed with them, so that they knew for sure the Lord Jesus was Christ the Savior.

> *So when the Samaritans came to him, they urged him to stay with them, and* ***he stayed two days****.*
>
> (JOHN 4:40)

A Testimony

The author has a son-in-law who owns a wholesale business of power tools, and they are very close to each other. Nevertheless the author does not like to interfere with the financial operations of his son-in-law. The author once told him about tithing but had no intention at all to impose it on him since to give tithe should be one's own financial management. The author made several appeals until the son-in-law was willing to do so. The author remembered that at the end of February 2018, when he met him, the son-in-law suddenly said, "Dad, God is so awesome." The author asked, "Why?" So, he explained that several days previously, he and his wife, the author's daughter, calculated their financial position at the end of 2017 comparing it with theirs at the end of 2016. And he was shocked because the surplus was so excessive.

The author was often asked to join in the discussion about their business. "Dad, you know that our monthly turnover is this much and our profit is this percent, so our monthly profit will be this much. Our cost is this big, so every month we will have this amount of net profit. Thus, in a year the profit will be X dollars, yet in fact it is so much more, Dad. I also wonder where all the money comes from. Even if our profit is doubled to 2X dollars, the surplus is still far beyond because we found the difference compared to last year has mounted up to 5X." And both of them, husband and wife, until this day cannot understand where the 5X amount of money comes from.

The author himself is not surprised because during his life, he gave tithe, then quitted, gave tithe again, and then stopped again. Later, he has started tithing again until now. The author also did not remember why he stopped, but by stopping then giving again, the author has learned and experienced the difference between whenever he gave tithes and whenever he did not.

The author belongs to them who often encourage and remind family, friends, and congregation to give their tithes. To what purpose? It is not to gain more money. No! But so that we can see the awesomeness and greatness of God. When we are sick and pray and then recover, we can argue a lot, "Well, yes, I am healed because the doctor is great" or "because the medical world is so advanced" or "because the medicine is efficacious" or "because the illness is not too serious." But, concerning giving tithes, there would not be too many arguments and disputes. Why? Because in economics we are taught that "if you want to have more money, then spend less." But the Lord told us to give, and we will receive more, and not just more, He even promised to give us abundantly by opening the windows of heaven for us.

> *"Bring the whole tithe into the storehouse, that there may be food in my house. Test me in this," says the Lord Almighty, "and see* ***if I will not throw open the floodgates of heaven and pour out so much blessing that there will not be room enough to store it.****"*
>
> (MALACHI 3:10)

The author speaks of tithing not because he wants to get the tithes while he is not a pastor or a minister, but rather that we ourselves can really feel the power of the Lord so as to experience and witness that the Lord we worship is the living God, the amazing, awesome great God!

Therefore, let us be doers of the Word, not just hearers, so that the solid foundations of the Christian faith we have could be manifested. This is what the Bible describes as having the living faith, and not the reverse, the dead faith if we are only hearers and not doers of the Word of God.

> *As the body without the spirit is dead, so faith without deeds is dead.*
>
> *(JAMES 2:26)*

The Characteristics of GOD's Children

Yunus Ciptawilangga, MBA

The Characteristics of God's Children

The Difference Between a "Christian" and a Child of God

If today we are called home by God, are we sure that we would go to Heaven?

We know that the ones who will go to Heaven are God's children, not merely people who like to go to church.

Therefore it is important for us to know whether we are God's children because if we turn out not to be His, then we will not go to Heaven; instead we will go to hell.

If we would like to know whether or not someone is a "Christian," it is not too difficult to find out. For example, we could take a look at his ID card or inquire if the person likes to go to church or not. If we want to be more certain, we can check whether the person is registered as a member of a church or even check whether or not he has been baptized.

However, it is not so easy to judge whether or not a person is a child of God. Indeed, the Bible records that God has put a mark on every child of God, but as humans we cannot see the mark. Likewise we cannot see the Holy Spirit who dwells in our hearts.

> *...set his seal of ownership on us, and put his Spirit in our hearts as a deposit, guaranteeing what is to come.*
>
> *(2 CORINTHIANS 1:22)*

If so, can't we know whether or not we are God's children?

Our Bible is marvelous. The Lord Jesus describes in detail the characteristics of God's children.

Let us read Matthew 7:21–23:

> *Matthew 7:21 Not everyone who says to me, 'Lord, Lord,' will enter the kingdom of heaven, but only the one who does the will of my Father who is in heaven.*
>
> *22 Many will say to me on that day, 'Lord, Lord, did we not prophesy in your name and in your name drive out demons and in your name perform many miracles?'*
>
> *23 Then I will tell them plainly, 'I never knew you. Away from me, you evildoers!'*

These three verses emphasize one thing in that verse 21 is repeated and explained further in verses 22–23.

If the Lord Jesus felt the need to repeat and explain it twice, then this was certainly an issue that the Lord Jesus took seriously.

We understand from reading verse 23, "Away from me, you evil-doers!" that these people were not allowed to enter the Kingdom of Heaven, or in other words they had to go to hell.

Let us analyze what kind of people they were.

From these verses it is clear that these people knew God or at least *thought they knew God* because if they did not know God, they could not call upon His name. (It is similar to instances when we see a stranger in a public place: we would not be able to say or call his name.)

The words "say" and "Lord, Lord" gave evidence that they did not only think they knew God. They even felt close to and intimate with God. (If we do not know someone very well, then chances are we would not call out to the person in a loud voice repeatedly. We would probably approach the person and call his name with a normal voice.)

Besides that, verse 22 explained that they said, "Lord, Lord, did we not prophesy in your name and in your name drive out demons and in your name perform many miracles?"

Apparently they not only felt close to God, but were considered as great people who have been used by God extraordinarily because they prophesied in the name of God, cast out demons in the name of God, and performed many miracles in the name of God. How fantastic!

The writer does not know if any of us have ever prophesied in the name of God, cast out demons in the name of God, and performed many miracles in the name of God.

Probably most of us have never done such things.

If they who were superb as such finally went to hell, then what about us?

If we examine, the actual key to why these people were denied entry to the Kingdom of Heaven is found in verse 23, "I never knew you."

From this verse we see that being God's children does not merely mean that we know and think of God as our Father, but more important is whether or not *God knows us and considers us as His children!*

Therefore if we want to know whether or not the Lord Jesus knows us and deems us as His own, we need to study the characteristics of people that are known to God.

The characteristics are described in John 10:1–16 in "The Good Shepherd."

> *John 10:1 Very truly I tell you Pharisees, anyone who* ***does not enter the sheep pen by the gate****, but climbs in by some other way, is a thief and a robber.*
>
> *2 The one who enters by the gate is the shepherd of the sheep.*
>
> *3 The gatekeeper opens the gate for him, and* ***the sheep listen to his voice****. He* ***calls his own sheep by name*** *and* ***leads them out****.*
>
> *4 When he has brought out all his own, he goes on ahead of them, and* ***his sheep follow him because they know his voice****.*
>
> *5 But they will never follow a stranger; in fact, they will run away from him because* ***they do not recognize a stranger's voice****.*
>
> *6 Jesus used this figure of speech, but the Pharisees did not understand what he was telling them.*

*7 Therefore Jesus said again, "**Very truly I tell you, I am the gate for the sheep.***

8 All who have come before me are thieves and robbers, but the sheep have not listened to them.

*9 **I am the gate; whoever enters through me will be saved.** They will come in and go out, and find pasture.*

*10 The thief comes only to steal and kill and destroy; **I have come that they may have life, and have it to the full.***

*11 **I am the good shepherd. The good shepherd lays down his life for the sheep.***

12 The hired hand is not the shepherd and does not own the sheep. So when he sees the wolf coming, he abandons the sheep and runs away. Then the wolf attacks the flock and scatters it.

13 The man runs away because he is a hired hand and cares nothing for the sheep.

*14 I am the good shepherd; **I know my sheep and my sheep know me—***

15 just as the Father knows me and I know the Father—and I lay down my life for the sheep.

16 ***I have other sheep that are not of this sheep pen****. I must bring them also. They too will listen to my voice, and* ***there shall be one flock and one shepherd.****"*

Just as there was a repetition in Matthew 7:21–23, there was also repetition in the Parable of the Good Shepherd in that verses 1–5 were repeated and explained in more detail in verses 7–16.

Verses 1–2:

Very truly I tell you Pharisees, anyone who ***does not enter the sheep pen by the gate****, but climbs in by some other way, is a thief and a robber.*

2 The one who enters by the gate is the shepherd of the sheep.

This is explained further in verses 7–11:

*7 Therefore Jesus said again, "****Very truly I tell you, I am the gate for the sheep.***

8 All who have come before me are thieves and robbers, but the sheep have not listened to them.

9 ***I am the gate; whoever enters through me will be saved****. They will come in and go out, and find pasture.*

10 The thief comes only to steal and kill and destroy; ***I have come that they may have life, and have it to the full.***

*11 **I am the good shepherd. The good shepherd lays down his life for the sheep.***

These verses explained about the "gate," that is, the gate to salvation. It was clearly stated that Jesus is the gate of salvation and those who claim to provide ways to salvation other than through Jesus (the gate) are just thieves and robbers (v. 1).

Why could Jesus be the only gate? Because Jesus and only Jesus died on the cross to give His life to redeem all mankind.

The good shepherd lays down his life for the sheep. (v. 11)

Furthermore:

*3 The gatekeeper opens the gate for him, and **the sheep listen to his voice**. He **calls his own sheep by name** and **leads them out**.*

*4 When he has brought out all his own, he goes on ahead of them, and **his sheep follow him because they know his voice**.*

*14 I am the good shepherd; **I know my sheep and my sheep know me**.*

The three verses above describe the following conditions:

1. God's children always listen to God's voice—"the sheep listen to his voice" (v. 3).
2. God knows His children and there are personal relationships

between God and His children—"He calls his own sheep by name"; "I know my sheep" (vv. 3, 14).

3. God will lead His children out of a worldly life—"(he) leads them out" (v. 3).
4. God's children do not only hear God's voice, but also follow God—"his sheep follow him" (v. 4).
5. God's children know the voice/Word of God and know God personally—"they know his voice"; "my sheep know me" (vv. 4, 14).

If we look at these characteristics of God's children, in that they listen to the voice/Word of God, have a personal relationship with God, are guided by God, follow God, and know the Word as well as the person of God, then, I think, the starting key to becoming a true child of God is by developing the fifth characteristic, which is "God's children know the voice/Word of God and know the person of God."

What is the meaning of knowing the Word of God and knowing the person of God?

To know the Word of God means to know all the laws and commandments of God, while to know the person of God is to know God as a person and to know all His character and greatness.

So *the first characteristic of a child of God is*:

We know the person of God and know His laws and commandments.

Do we know God and all His laws and commandments?

Let us get some examples:

God is all-loving:

Your love, Lord, reaches to the heavens, your faithfulness to the skies.

(Psalm 36:5)

Remember, Lord, your great mercy and love, for they are from of old.

(Psalm 25:6)

For I am convinced that neither death nor life, neither angels nor demons, neither the present nor the future, nor any powers.

(Romans 8:38)

...neither height nor depth, nor anything else in all creation, will be able to separate us from the love of God that is in Christ Jesus our Lord.

(Romans 8:39)

What is God's great love like? Does that mean we may commit sin at will because God will certainly forgive?

God is also gracious.

For his anger lasts only a moment, but his favor lasts a lifetime; weeping may stay for the night, but rejoicing comes in the morning.

(Psalm 30:5)

Be merciful, just as your Father is merciful.

(Luke 6:36)

What is the generous God like? Since God is generous, can we assume that God is easygoing and so we dare to enter a church which is "God's house" with any appearance and attitude at will? Dare we eat and drink in church, chat, and even play games in God's House?

Our God is the most holy:

But the Lord Almighty will be exalted by his justice, and the holy God will be proved holy by his righteous acts.

(ISAIAH 5:16)

How should we respond to God's holiness?

1 Peter 1:14 As obedient children, do not conform to the evil desires you had when you lived in ignorance.

15 But just as he who called you is holy, so be holy in all you do;

16 for it is written: "Be holy, because I am holy."

17 Since you call on a Father who judges each person's work impartially, live out your time as foreigners here in reverent fear.

18 For you know that it was not with perishable things such as silver or gold that you were redeemed from the empty way of life handed down to you from your ancestors,

19 but with the precious blood of Christ, a lamb without blemish or defect.

Besides the many other attributes of God, we also need to know all the laws and commandments of God.

For instance, how our attitude should be when we enter God's house:

Therefore, since we are receiving a kingdom that cannot be shaken, let us be thankful, and so worship God acceptably with reverence and awe.

(HEBREWS 12:28)

What a ministry is and how our attitude and performance toward a ministry should be:

1 Peter 4:10 Each of you should use whatever gift you have received to serve others, as faithful stewards of God's grace in its various forms.

11 If anyone speaks, they should do so as one who speaks the very words of God. If anyone serves, they should do so with the strength God provides, so that in all things God may be praised through Jesus Christ. To him be the glory and the power for ever and ever. Amen.

What the most important task is that the Lord commanded us to do as long as we live in this world:

Ecclesiastes 12:13 Now all has been heard; here is the conclusion of the matter: Fear God and keep his commandments, for this is the duty of all mankind.

14 For God will bring every deed into judgment, including every hidden thing, whether it is good or evil.

How we should live our lives as God's children:

Therefore, my dear friends, as you have always obeyed—not only in my presence, but now much more in my absence—continue to work out your salvation with fear and trembling.

(PHILIPPIANS 2:12)

Are all food "clean" in God's eyes for us to eat? (Are we allowed by God to eat all kinds food?)

Mark 7:18 "Are you so dull?" he asked. "Don't you see that nothing that enters a person from the outside can defile them?

19 For it doesn't go into their heart but into their stomach, and then out of the body." (In saying this, Jesus declared all foods clean.)

And there are still so many laws of God and God's other commandments that we must understand.

Probably quite a lot of us feel that we have already known God and His laws and commandments.

To what extent do we have to get to know God and His laws and commandments?

> *But they will never follow a stranger; in fact, they will run away from him because **they do not recognize a stranger's voice**.*
>
> *(JOHN 10:5)*

The above verse explains that we should study the person of God and His laws and commandments until we can distinguish between God's laws and commandments and those that are not His, or, in other words, until we can distinguish between the Word of God and those that are not of God, between God's teachings and heresies.

Why should we reach that level of understanding to be able to distinguish between the Word and heresies?

Because God knows that there are a great number of false prophets and teachings that will mislead a vast number of God's children, especially in these last days.

> *Watch out for false prophets. They come to you in sheep's clothing, but inwardly they are ferocious wolves.*
>
> *(MATTHEW 7:15)*

> *...and many false prophets will appear and deceive many people.*
>
> *(MATTHEW 24:11)*

> *For false messiahs and false prophets will appear and perform great signs and wonders to deceive, if possible, even the elect.*
>
> *(MATTHEW 24:24)*

How can we get to know the person of God and all His laws and commandments?

We can know God and His laws and commandments from sermons delivered by His servant. Therefore, we must prepare our hearts to listen carefully to His Words and earnestly pray to God that the Holy Spirit would guide us and give us understanding.

1 Corinthians 2:10 these are the things God has revealed to us by his Spirit. The Spirit searches all things, even the deep things of God.

11 For who knows a person's thoughts except their own spirit within them? In the same way no one knows the thoughts of God except the Spirit of God.

12 What we have received is not the spirit of the world, but the Spirit who is from God, so that we may understand what God has freely given us.

13 This is what we speak, not in words taught us by human wisdom but in words taught by the Spirit, explaining spiritual realities with Spirit-taught words.

14 The person without the Spirit does not accept the things that come from the Spirit of God but considers them foolishness, and cannot understand them because they are discerned only through the Spirit.

15 The person with the Spirit makes judgments about all things, but such a person is not subject to merely human judgments,

We can also learn how to get to know the person of God and all His laws and commandments in a deeper way from books. The best book to study is the Bible because information from and about God and all His laws and commandments are contained in His Word.

We do not need to worry if we do not understand everything because as described in 1 Corinthians 2 above, if we are God's children, the Spirit of God Himself will explain to us even the things that are hidden in God.

How should we read the Bible?

We need to read the Bible from "Genesis to Revelation" without skipping any section.

Why should we read from Genesis to Revelation?

Because the Bible is a unity.

Why is it that we should not skip reading any part of the Bible?

Because there is not one verse, word, or even punctuation that is meaningless.

From the first description of the characteristics of God's children, we understand that their development is not determined by how long we have been going to church, or how often we have gone to church, how active we are in church, nor how much we give financially. It does not matter how high our positions are in church, *instead, it is determined by how deep we know God and His laws and commandments*.

I remember that when I was a teenager, there was a saying "people who know the Lord" used as a description for God's children, not just people who had been to church, but those who have come to know the Lord.

We are God's children and God is our Father:

The Spirit you received does not make you slaves, so that you live in fear again; rather, the Spirit you received brought about your adoption to sonship. And by him we cry, "Abba, Father."

(ROMANS 8:15)

As children of God, of course, brings the responsibility to know God the Father. Hence, it is questionable if we as children of the Father do not know Him and do not have the desire to get to know our Father better.

We often hear many stories of abandoned children who strive to find and get to know their parents.

I once watched a movie about a girl who lived with her mother in Vietnam. She tried to find her Korean father. The child left Vietnam for unfamiliar Korea, to look for her father. He sought out her father, not to hold him accountable but just to see her father's face.

If we consider ourselves to be "God's children," is there any desire to get to know our God who is our Father? Do we desire to read the Bible and to contemplate and implement His Word in our lives?

Blessed is the one who does not walk in step with the wicked or stand in the way that sinners take or sit in the company of mockers, but whose delight is in the law of the Lord, and who meditates on his law day and night.

(PSALM 1:1,2)

On my bed I remember you; I think of you through the watches of the night.

Because you are my help, I sing in the shadow of your wings.

(Psalm 63:6,7)

Cause me to understand the way of your precepts, that I may meditate on your wonderful deeds.

(Psalm 119:27)

What is more, I consider everything a loss because of the surpassing worth of knowing Christ Jesus my Lord, for whose sake I have lost all things. I consider them garbage, that I may gain Christ.

(Philippians 3:8)

But grow in the grace and knowledge of our Lord and Savior Jesus Christ. To him be glory both now and forever! Amen.

(2 Peter 3:18)

If until now we do not have a desire to get to know the Father and there is no desire to read the Bible, we should ask ourselves, "Is it true that I am a child of God?" Or do we actually *just feel* that we are God's children like those people who call Lord, Lord? Or in simple terminology, could it be that actually we are only *church visitors* because how would it be possible that we are God's children if we do not have any desire to know God?

God's children must know God and that all of God's laws and commandments have been delivered by the Lord Jesus on other occasions; for example:

But seek first his kingdom and his righteousness, and all these things will be given to you as well.

(MATTHEW 6:33)

The kingdom of God is God and all His greatness, whereas His righteousness is God's laws and commandments. Only God's laws and commandments are true, nothing else.

The phrase "seek first his kingdom and his righteousness" means that we *give priority* to knowing God and all His laws and commandments. God will add what we need when we come to know Him and all His laws and commandments "and all these things will be given to you as well."

In the Old Testament, "to know God and His laws and commandments" was described as "to fear God."

And now, Israel, what does the Lord your God ask of you but to fear the Lord your God, to walk in obedience to him, to love him, to serve the Lord your God with all your heart and with all your soul.

(DEUTERONOMY 10:12)

Assemble the people—men, women and children, and the foreigners residing in your towns—so they can listen and learn to fear the Lord your God and follow carefully all the words of this law.

(DEUTERONOMY 31:12)

What does to fear God mean?

If the writer may make a comparison, what is the meaning of "to fear the police"?

To fear the police constitute three requirements, namely:

1. We have to know the characteristics of the police: How can we fear the police if we do not know what the police are like, because not all who wear a uniform are policemen. We know that members of certain mass organizations wear uniforms, such as members of the armed forces, for instance.
2. We have to know the traffic signs, laws, and regulations and understand the instructions of the police.
3. We have to be obedient: After we understand the police and their rules, we obey their orders.

Likewise the fear of God starts with knowing God, understanding all His laws and commandments, and obeying them. How would it be possible for us to obey when we do not know God and His laws and commandments?

The second characteristic of God's children is that they follow the Lord—"his sheep follow him."

What is the meaning of following God?

Following God means not to follow our own desires but to follow the will of God.

What are our desires? Our desires are the desires of the flesh, namely:

Galatians 5:19 The acts of the flesh are obvious: sexual immorality, impurity and debauchery;

20 idolatry and witchcraft; hatred, discord, jealousy, fits of rage, selfish ambition, dissensions, factions

21 and envy; drunkenness, orgies, and the like. I warn you, as I did before, that those who live like this ***will not inherit the kingdom of God.***

It means that when we, as God's children, still do things like the above, there is no change in our lives. Before becoming a Christian, we committed adultery; now after becoming a Christian, we still commit adultery; before, we worshipped idols; now we still worship idols; before, we often disagree; now we still often disagree; before, we got drunk; now, we still get drunk; and so on. It is very likely that we are not God's children although we attend church. Since we have not become followers of Christ, verse 21 warns that we "will not inherit the kingdom of God."

Why can we not enter the kingdom of God and go to hell? Because if we are still living in the flesh, then we are not God's children. Once we accept Jesus as our Lord and Savior at that moment, we have died to sin.

Romans 6:1 What shall we say, then? Shall we go on sinning so that grace may increase?

2 By no means! We are those who have died to sin; how can we live in it any longer?

3 Or don't you know that all of us who were baptized into Christ Jesus were baptized into his death?

4 We were therefore buried with him through baptism into death in order that, just as Christ was raised from the dead through the glory of the Father, we too may live a new life.

5 For if we have been united with him in a death like his, we will certainly also be united with him in a resurrection like his.

6 For we know that our old self was crucified with him so that the body ruled by sin might be done away with, that we should no longer be slaves to sin—

7 because anyone who has died has been set free from sin.

8 Now if we died with Christ, we believe that we will also live with him.

9 For we know that since Christ was raised from the dead, he cannot die again; death no longer has mastery over him.

10 The death he died, he died to sin once for all; but the life he lives, he lives to God.

11 In the same way, count yourselves dead to sin but alive to God in Christ Jesus.

12 Therefore do not let sin reign in your mortal body so that you obey its evil desires.

13 Do not offer any part of yourself to sin as an instrument of wickedness, but rather offer yourselves to God as those who have been brought from death to life; and offer every part of yourself to him as an instrument of righteousness.

14 For sin shall no longer be your master, because you are not under the law, but under grace.

15 What then? Shall we sin because we are not under the law but under grace? By no means!

16 Don't you know that when you offer yourselves to someone as obedient slaves, you are slaves of the one you obey—whether you are slaves to sin, which leads to death, or to obedience, which leads to righteousness?

17 But thanks be to God that, though you used to be slaves to sin, you have come to obey from your heart the pattern of teaching that has now claimed your allegiance.

18 You have been set free from sin and have become slaves to righteousness.

19 I am using an example from everyday life because of your human limitations. Just as you used to offer yourselves as slaves to impurity and to ever-increasing wickedness, so now offer yourselves as slaves to righteousness leading to holiness.

20 When you were slaves to sin, you were free from the control of righteousness.

21 What benefit did you reap at that time from the things you are now ashamed of? Those things result in death!

22 But now that you have been set free from sin and have become slaves of God, the benefit you reap leads to holiness, and the result is eternal life.

23 For the wages of sin is death, but the gift of God is eternal life in Christ Jesus our Lord.

Following God means following God's will, that is, living according to the leading of the Spirit to produce the fruit of the Spirit.

Galatians 5:22 But the fruit of the Spirit is love, joy, peace, forbearance, kindness, goodness, faithfulness,

23 gentleness and self-control. Against such things there is no law.

24 Those who belong to Christ Jesus have crucified the flesh with its passions and desires.

25 Since we live by the Spirit, let us keep in step with the Spirit.

26 Let us not become conceited, provoking and envying each other.

When we follow Christ, we will listen to God's Word and do it in our lives. It is indeed not an easy thing to do the Word of God. Just as the sheep are commanded by shepherds to immediately return to the stable, even though they may not be full or still want to dry themselves or are still tired, they will still follow their shepherd's voice.

Likewise, we will learn to obey to do the Word of God because our faith is expressed by obedience we do the Lord's command:

> *In the same way, faith by itself, if it is not accompanied by action, is dead.* (James 2:17)

We may have a husband who has rude behavior and likes to be distracted, unfaithful, and less responsible as a husband or as a father. However, we will still bow and respect our husbands because we want to obey God's command:

> *Wives, submit yourselves to your own husbands as you do to the Lord.*
>
> (EPHESIANS 5:22)

Likewise, we might have a wife who is fussy, unwise, quarrelsome, and far from ideal. However, we will continue to love our wives because it is God's command:

> *Husbands, love your wives, just as Christ loved the church and gave himself up for her.*
>
> (EPHESIANS 5:25)

Our economy may not be well established and there are still many needs that have not been fulfilled. However, we will continue to pay taxes and tithe properly because we want to be obedient children of God:

He said to them, "Then give back to Caesar what is Caesar's, and to God what is God's."

(LUKE 20:25)

The third characteristic of God's children is that they have a personal relationship with God—"He calls his own sheep by name."

Christianity is not about doing rituals, instead it is a personal relationship with God. Before the fall into sin, men had a very personal relationship with God, but sin broke that relationship: men were cast out from the presence of God.

The Lord Jesus died on the cross to pay for our sins so that we can be reconciled back to God have a personal relationship with Him again.

God presented Christ as a sacrifice of atonement, through the shedding of his blood—to be received by faith. He did this to demonstrate his righteousness, because in his forbearance he had left the sins committed beforehand unpunished.

(ROMANS 3:25)

Therefore a child of God will have a desire to come close to God. He will make time for devotions and routine prayers. Additionally, a child of God will also feel a personal connection with God. Not only will we talk to God through our prayers, but we also will experience

God's answers to our prayers. We will see and feel how God's power is manifested in our lives, like a child who sees the abilities of his father in solving many problems.

Hence our personal relationship with God becomes one of the characteristics and the basis of our faith. Many Christians have been amazed by another's testimony. This is not bad, but we should not base our faith on the testimony of others, whoever he is and no matter how great his testimony is, because our faith must be based on our personal relationship with God as experienced by Job and the Samaritans:

> *My ears had heard of you but now my eyes have seen you. (Job 42:5)*

> *They said to the woman, "We no longer believe just because of what you said; now we have heard for ourselves, and we know that this man really is the Savior of the world."*
>
> *(JOHN 4:42)*

The fourth characteristic of God's children is that we feel God's guidance to be like Jesus Christ in every step of our lives—"(he) leads them out."

All this time, do we feel the guidance of God bringing us out of a mundane life to be like Jesus Christ?

If we have never felt God's guidance and feel that we walk alone in this world, then we ought to check our status. Because just as much as parents will continue to guide their children to develop into good and healthy children, so does God continually guide us that we may become more and more acceptable to Him, that is, to be like the Lord Jesus Christ.

For those God foreknew he also predestined to be conformed to the image of his Son, that he might be the firstborn among many brothers and sisters.

(ROMANS 8:29)

If we go back to Matthew 7:21–23:

21 Not everyone who says to me, 'Lord, Lord,' will enter the kingdom of heaven, but only the one who does the will of my Father who is in heaven.

22 Many will say to me on that day, 'Lord, Lord, did we not prophesy in your name and in your name drive out demons and in your name perform many miracles?'

23 Then I will tell them plainly, 'I never knew you. Away from me, you evildoers!'

These verses can be explained as follows:

1. Not all who call or even cried Lord, Lord, are God's children, and therefore there is no certainty that they will enter the Kingdom of Heaven.
2. Those who do the will of the Father (and thus known by Jesus), know God, know the laws of God, and obey the will of God will enter Heaven.
3. Serving God, even in marvelous ways like prophesying, casting out demons, and performing many miracles, is not the main characteristic of God's children. Everyone can do that

by saying the name of the true God because the power lies in the "name of God"—not in the person doing it.

"Teacher," said John, "we saw someone driving out demons in your name and we told him to stop, because he was not one of us."

(Mark 9:38)

Similar to an incident where a police officer shot a man to death, the powerful aspect was the pistol, not the police, because if the gun was fired by an amateur but the bullet hit the vital part of one's body, the victim can die, too.

4. A child of God is a person known by God.
5. Any person who is not a child of God, however great or good the person is, is basically an evildoer because he did not receive the forgiveness of sins from God through the Lord Jesus Christ.

Observe the Great Commission from the Lord Jesus in Matthew 28:19–20:

19 Therefore go and make disciples of all nations, baptizing them in the name of the Father and of the Son and of the Holy Spirit,

20 and teaching them to obey everything I have commanded you. And surely I am with you always, to the very end of the age.

It is clearly conveyed that we have to "teach all nations" to make them *His disciples*.

The term "disciples" is related with "learning" and "teaching" activities. Learning and teaching what?

Learning and teaching "everything I have commanded you."

What are they? To know God and to know all the laws and commandments of God.

And then "teaching them to obey" (everything I have commanded you).

In the last days before the return of the Lord Jesus, let each one of us check ourselves to make sure that we are truly God's children. Let us sincerely learn to be God-fearing people and read more of the Bible while we have the time and the chance to do it, as this beautiful opportunity will not always be available. Let us set up a time for meditating and conducting family worship as well.

4 Types Of Christians

Yunus Ciptawilangga, MBA

Four Types of Christians

Preface

Actually the writer has no plan to write this book about *Four Types of Christians* since this material was already discussed in a simple way in the writer's book entitled *The Rapture, Fulfillment of: The Signs in the Sky, the Festivals in Summer, and the Parable of the End Times Part I.*

However, early last August when the writer was making his final preparation to preach at one of the churches in Bandung, the writer's interest was diverted to change the prepared material for his message with *The Parable of the Sower*. The next day he conveyed this message under the title *Faith and Wealth.*

The writer was surprised when shaking hands with the congregation at the end of the service; quite a lot of people thanked him for the sermon he had delivered. Likewise, it occurred when the material was delivered in another church. Therefore the writer decided to write down this material as a book.

In this book the subject of the Christians' responsibility to pay tax is also discussed:

Then Jesus said to them, "Give back to Caesar what is Caesar's and to God what is God's."

(Mark 12:17a)

Paying tax has been the writer's struggle since the year 2000. And the Word of God regarding these *Four Types of Christians* is actually one of God's ways to encourage the writer to pay tax honestly and properly.

Truly, our God is so good that He continually reminds and guides us so as to live Christlike.

Whoever claims to live in him must live as Jesus did.

(1 John 2:6)

Finally, all the glory is to God who gives us all the wisdom and bestows us His mercy.

But we have this treasure in jars of clay to show that this all-surpassing power is from God and not from us.

(2 Corinthians 4:7)

Soli Deo Gloria,
The writer

Four Types of Christians

Let us read Matthew 13:1–9 and 18–23:

13:1 That same day Jesus went out of the house and sat by the lake.

2 Such large crowds gathered around him that he got into a boat and sat in it, while all the people stood on the shore.

3 Then he told them many things in parables, saying: "A farmer went out to sow his seed.

4 As he was scattering the seed, some fell along the path, and the birds came and ate it up.

5 Some fell on rocky places, where it did not have much soil. It sprang up quickly, because the soil was shallow.

6 But when the sun came up, the plants were scorched, and they withered because they had no root.

7 Other seed fell among thorns, which grew up and choked the plants.

8 Still other seed fell on good soil, where it produced a crop—a hundred, sixty or thirty times what was sown.

9 Whoever has ears, let them hear.

13:18 Listen then to what the parable of the sower means:

19 When anyone hears the message about the kingdom and does not understand it, the evil one comes and snatches away what was sown in their heart. This is the seed sown along the path.

20 The seed falling on rocky ground refers to someone who hears the word and at once receives it with joy.

21 But since they have no root, they last only a short time. When trouble or persecution comes because of the word, they quickly fall away.

22 The seed falling among the thorns refers to someone who hears the word, but the worries of this life and the deceitfulness of wealth choke the word, making it unfruitful.

23 But the seed falling on good soil refers to someone who hears the word and understands it. This is the one who produces a crop, yielding a hundred, sixty or thirty times what was sown.

The Parable of the Sower explains about four types of Christians:

First Type of Christians

The first type of Christians are described in Matthew 13:4 as follows:

As he was scattering the seed, some fell along the path, and the birds came and ate it up.

And the explanation is found in verse 19:

When anyone hears the message about the kingdom and does not understand it, the evil one comes and snatches away what was sown in their heart. This is the seed sown along the path.

This first type of Christians are those who have been evangelized, but they do not really understand; they do not get the meaning of the message shared. They don't understand the meaning of salvation in Christ. Thus, *they cannot be considered as God's children.* They might feel as God's children, in their ID cards, they are recognized as Christians, they might be valid members of a church, their parents might be Christians, and even their father might be a pastor. Yet they actually did not understand about salvation. They did not really get the true meaning of being saved in Christ.

So, this first type Christians are actually not God's children. They have not yet become God's children.

Romans 10:9 explains about salvation:

*If you **declare** with your mouth, "Jesus is Lord," and **believe** in your heart that God raised him from the dead, you will be saved.*

To declare has the connotation of "being conscious" or "in a conscious condition." One has to be conscious when he or she makes a confession. That is why in the statements or letters of confession, it is always written underneath: "I write this statement/acknowledgment in a conscious condition, without any pressure and in a healthy condition." Thus, when someone is considered unconscious, whatever he or she conveys cannot be validated as a legal statement or legal acknowledgment.

Likewise, the word "believe" implies a connotation of "understand." We cannot believe something we do not understand.

The writer's grandson once asked, "Grandpa, which one is bigger, the sun or the moon?" "The sun," the writer answered. "But the moon looks bigger," he responded. The writer explained, "The sun looks small because it is further away from us. Grandpa will give you an example." The writer took a book and continued his explanation, "Now, keep looking at this book." Then the writer walked backward, further backward, and still further. Then he asked, "As you keep watching, the book looks smaller and smaller, doesn't it? So is it with the sun and the moon. The sun looks smaller because it is further away from the earth or from us than the moon. If their distance from the earth is the same, the sun will look much bigger." Finally the kid understood though may be not completely or not hundred percent. Yet he has already gotten the picture. One must first understand before he can believe.

Now, there is something important here, namely, that we need to introspect ourselves: Have we ever consciously accepted Christ as our personal Lord and Savior and with true understanding? Our parents might have dedicated us to the Lord when we were still babies or children, and we were baptized as teenagers. But let us recall from our memory whether at that time we were fully conscious and understood because if we were not fully conscious or not really aware and did not fully understand, we *might not have become Christians yet or might not have become God's children. Why so?* Because we have never received Christ as Lord and Savior consciously and with true understanding.

Second Type of Christians

Then about the second type of Christians, it is said in Matthew 13:5,6:

> *Some fell on rocky places, where it did not have much soil. It sprang up quickly, because the soil was shallow. But when the sun came up, the plants were scorched, and they withered because they had no root.*

Luke 8:6 explains about this second type of Christians:

> *Some fell on rocky ground, and when it came up, the plants withered because they* ***had no moisture****.*

In Matthew 13:20,21, the meaning of this second type of Christians is also explained:

> *The seed falling on rocky ground refers to someone who hears the word and* ***at once receives it with joy****. But* ***since they have no root****, they last only a short time. When trouble or persecution comes because of the word,* ***they quickly fall away****.*

So this second type of Christians are those who accept Christ after being evangelized *and become children of God, but they do not keep their faith*. Their faith is never "watered" (nourished). When they have just received Christ as Lord and Savior, they went diligently to church. Yet, by and by they will not go to the church anymore. Perhaps they liked to pray, but by and by, they never pray anymore. They liked to read the Bible, but by and by, they never read it anymore. Perhaps they used to serve, but by and by, they never serve anymore. They do not maintain their faith. And about this second type of Christians, it is clearly stated that "When trouble or persecution comes because of the Word, *he quickly falls away*."

Some of them who hear the Word of God are sensitive to what is good, but they keep the Word only in their minds, not in their hearts. They do not put God's Word into practice during their lives. Their Christian lives are merely following the religious rituals and they are not rooted in the Word. As a result, when everything goes well, they maintain in their faith, but when they face difficulties and persecutions, they give up their belief and leave to follow other beliefs.

Third Type of Christians

Matthew 13:7 says:

> *Other seed fell among thorns, which grew up and choked the plants.*

> *The seed falling among the thorns refers to someone who hears the word, but the worries of this life and the deceitfulness of wealth choke the word, making it unfruitful. (Matthew 13:22)*

The third type of Christians are people who *accept Christ as their Lord and Savior and their faith has grown*, yet there are thorns. Thorns or thornbush also grow, and we know that thorns grow faster than rice plants or wheat. *Finally the thornbush will press and choke the other plants so they will die and do not have the chance to produce any fruit.*

John 15:2 says, "***He cuts off every branch in me that bears no***

***fruit**, while every branch that does bear fruit he prunes so that it will be even more fruitful.*"

Thornbush and Other Prickly Shrubs

We will discuss about these thornbush and prickly shrubs. Matthew 13:7 states:

> *Other seed fell among thorns, which grew up and choked the plants.*

> *The seed falling among the thorns refers to someone who hears the word, but the worries of this life and the deceitfulness of wealth choke the word, making it unfruitful.*
>
> *(MATTHEW 13:22)*

What do the thorns in these verses mean? Thorns or thornbush here represent worldly worries and deceptions of wealth. According to Mark 4:19:

> *...but **the worries of this life, the deceitfulness of wealth** and **the desires for other things** come in and choke the word, making it unfruitful.*

In Mark, it is mentioned more clearly that thornbush illustrates the *worries of this life* and *the deceitfulness of wealth* and *the desires for other things* or *the desires of the flesh*. We will discuss them one by one.

1. The Worries of This Life

The worries of this life are the cares of this world. We worry and are very much concerned about our future, our advanced or old age, the fate of our children and grandchildren, and even what to eat today and tomorrow.

However, the Bible explains that during the forty years the Israelites wandered in the wilderness, God had kept them and provided for their needs. Also Elijah was taken care of, and every day the Lord told the crows to bring bread and meat for him. Likewise in the case of the five loaves and the two fish, the Lord could use those to feed five thousand people.

Now some would say, "Of course, Sir. But that was in the past. Today, it is different."

But the Lord promises to provide for us. Matthew 6:31–32 says:

31 So do not worry, saying, 'What shall we eat?' or 'What shall we drink?' or 'What shall we wear?'

32 For the pagans run after all these things, and your heavenly Father knows that you need them.

1 Peter 5:7 emphasizes this:

Cast all your anxiety on him because he cares for you.

Some might say, "Sir, I also believe those verses, but honestly my faith is weak, and I am not sure whether the Lord would or would not provide for me." And some others might say, "I believe that God would provide for His children. But I have so many sins, Sir, so I am not sure whether the Lord will provide for me."

What does it mean?

There are many reasons for people not to believe in the Lord. Instead, they believe more in their fellowmen and in their wealth: "Here Sir, our wealth and family can assure or guarantee the maintenance of my present life even until my advanced age."

2. The Deceitfulness of Wealth

We know that these days we live in a world where people live glamorously or extravagantly. Watching the TV we will hear whose mansion is the most grandiose, who owns a private airplane, has luxurious cars, and so on. And in the news we hear of B or C who has just bought a new luxurious ship. Some actresses or actors or celebrities spend their holidays in Paris and stay in some expensive luxurious international hotels of ten thousands US dollars for one night. They dine in costly famous restaurants where delicious food is served, prepared by well-known chefs. The daily accessories they wear are among others: branded bags of a hundred thousand US dollars and famous watch special edition of a million dollars. And some more details are told about their shopping tours and fantastic expenses for items of famous brands.

Not only celebrities, every day we too see our friends via WhatsApp. Perhaps they are spending their holidays somewhere, or some of them are enjoying special delicacies in well-known restaurants, clad in beautiful dresses. "Wow, our relative changes his car, and our friend buys a new gadget." Hence every day we see and are entertained by such news and may think how happy their lives are!

That is why we naturally wish to be rich, for if we were rich, we could enjoy such conspicuous entertainments. Are we allowed to be rich? Sure. Why not? Abraham was rich and David too. Yet we should be careful not to become like the third type of Christians who own at least these characteristics:

Money Is the Standard

1 Timothy 6:10 records that:

> *For the love of money is a root of all kinds of evil. Some people, eager for money, have wandered from the faith and pierced themselves with many griefs.*

The verse is always there as a reminder, but many people still think that money is the most important subject, for money is assumed as an insurance of one's future and their happiness in this world. That is why this third type of Christians usually measure everything with money. Their standard is money. When they are introduced to a new person who is good and religious and who speaks gently and politely, they might not welcome him readily because they think, "This person is good, but is he or she beneficial and would bring in money? Is he or she materially advantageous? If not, they would not be interested to have any relationship with him or her. On the other hand, when they are introduced to another person who is a real brute, lascivious, drunkard, addicted to drugs, and so on, they welcome him with open arms because such individual can bring in material advantages. The standard is whoever can bring in money, not whoever can bring in virtue or moral excellence to them.

Even in the Family, Money Is the Standard

There is a family that has a good character child. When they are sick, he/she would come over and take them to the hospital. But if they need money, he/she cannot give much since economically his/her financial resources are not so good. And oftentimes they deem such a child defective or a failure, unlike the other son, whose character is not so attentive, never visits them even when they are sick, yet sends them a good sum of money, who they consider to be a devoted child.

There are also good husbands, who are faithful and love their wives, but they are not respected by their wives because they cannot earn much money. The writer even witnessed a wife who dared to disgrace her husband openly because she earned more. Did she know that she was obliged to submit to her husband and to obey him? She knew, but she answered, "I will obey my husband if he earns more than I do. But as it is now, most of the family expenses are on my responsibility. So, why should I obey him? If he wants me to obey him, he must be able to earn more than I do. Then sure enough, I shall obey him."

Now, what does this mean?

The standard in the family is no more the Bible, but the content of the purse: money.

The Way to Get Money

It is apparent in the way they get money. They who belong to this third type of Christians love money: when they seek for money, they do not mind the means or the way to get it—fair or foul. Their principle is "by hook or by crook since money is odorless." Any means is permissible—to bribe, to cheat, to exploit, to manipulate—because the most important thing to them is to obtain money!

Does Not Want to Help Their Relatives

Christians of this type also rarely help their kinfolk or relatives. They usually will reflect carefully whether helping their relatives would be beneficial. When it would be beneficial, they probably will help them; if not, they will not help them.

1 Timothy 5:8 says:

> *Anyone who does not provide for their relatives, and especially for their own household, has denied the faith and is worse than an unbeliever.*

3. The Desires for Other Things

The desires for other things mean more like living in the flesh. They are children of God who do not want to bear the cross.

In Matthew 16:24 the Lord Jesus clearly said:

> *Then Jesus said to his disciples, "Whoever wants to be my disciple must deny themselves and take up their cross and follow me."*

At the moment we decide to follow Jesus Christ, He wants us to deny ourselves and learn to live a holy life.

Some people often say, "It is not that I refuse to live a holy life, but at present I cannot since I am still in this business. If I do not go with them to the night club and do not play with the girls there, those people will reject me and I will not get any orders. In my business, if I do not cheat nor manipulate, the price I offered would not be satisfactory. In short, please not now, Sir. Maybe later."

However, in this matter it is not a concern of incapability, rather they enjoy a sinful life:

And whoever does not carry their cross and follow me cannot be my disciple.

(LUKE 14:27)

The Danger of Becoming Christians of the Third Type

Changing One's Belief for Wealth

Matthew 6:24 clearly explains:

No one can serve two masters. Either you will hate the one and love the other, or you will be devoted to the one and despise the other. You cannot serve both God and money.

(NIV)

No man can serve two masters: for either he will hate the one, and love the other; or else he will hold to the one, and despise the other. Ye cannot serve God and mammon.

(KJV)

When we tend to love money/mammon, at that very moment, we have pushed away the Lord. We can never love both. We can choose but one. When we love the Lord more, we certainly do not love mammon.

On the other hand, when we love mammon more, we certainly do not love the Lord. The choice should be only one.

Further, Luke 12:15 admonishes us:

> *Then he said to them, "Watch out! Be on your guard against all kinds of greed; life does not consist in an abundance of possessions."*

Do not be deceived; do not think that if we have much money, we will be kept safe. No, not at all.

The greatest danger concerning the third type of Christians is they do not put in practice the Word of God. This makes their lives unfruitful, while the Lord Jesus clearly said that:

> ***He cuts off every branch in me that bears no fruit**, while every branch that does bear fruit he prunes so that it will be even more fruitful.*
>
> (JOHN 15:2)

Why should the "unfruitful" be cut off? Well, it is because they actually do not sincerely believe in the Lord! They are the people described in 2 Timothy 3:5 below:

> *...having a form of godliness but denying its power. Have nothing to do with such people.*

The Fourth Type of Christians

The fourth type of Christian are described in the following:

> *Still other seed fell on good soil, where it produced a crop—a hundred, sixty or thirty times what was sown.*
>
> *(MATTHEW 13:8)*

> *But the seed falling on good soil refers to someone who hears the word and* ***understands*** *it.* ***This is the one who produces a crop****, yielding a hundred, sixty or thirty times what was sown.*
>
> *(MATTHEW 13:23)*

> *But the seed on good soil stands for* ***those with a noble and good heart,*** *who hear the word,* ***retain it, and by persevering produce a crop****.*
>
> *(LUKE 8:15)*

Hence Christians of this fourth type are Christians who *not only listen* to God's Word but also *understand* and keep it in their hearts, as well as *fervently practice* it in their lives so that it bears fruit.

It is very interesting that in Matthew 13:23, the word "understand" precedes "produces a crop": "someone who hears the Word and *understands* it. *This is the one who produces a crop*" implies that we can bear fruit only if we understand. Hence, *understanding* the Word of God is one of the keys to be able to become a Christian of the fourth type who are fruitful.

Christians Who Understand the Word of God

As Christians, we often presume that we "understand the Word of God" because we have been God's children for quite a long time. However, the length of time we have been Christians does not guarantee that we would surely understand the Word of God. We often see people in the congregation doze off, busy with their gadgets or mobiles, chatting, no concentration, and their minds wandering far away while the sermon is being delivered. And even some activists in the church leave the auditorium when the sermons are being conveyed. Also many Christians never finish reading through the whole Bible, from the Book of Genesis to the Book of Revelation, even once! And some members of the Church Council and elders have finished reading it through but a few times. Indeed, there is no guarantee that they who have read through the Bible many times would definitely have more understanding. Yet one of the means to gain better understanding of the Word of God is to read the Bible other than listening to sermons.

Back to Matthew 13:23:

> *But the seed falling on good soil refers to someone who hears the word and* ***understands*** *it.* ***This is the one who produces a crop****, yielding a hundred, sixty or thirty times what was sown.*

Thus, we can bear fruit only if we have understood!

The Fourth Type of Christians and Their Wealth

What are the characteristics of these fourth type of Christians in managing their wealth?

In Luke 19:8 we read:

> *But Zacchaeus stood up and said to the Lord, "Look, Lord! **Here and now I give half of my possessions to the poor, and if I have cheated anybody out of anything, I will pay back four times the amount.**"*

There are three things Zacchaeus did after he repented.

First, when he met the Lord Jesus, he said, "Look, Lord! Here and now I give half of my possessions to the poor."

Why was Zacchaeus willing to give half of his wealth to the poor? Because he had found something more valuable than his wealth. When he received the Lord Jesus as his Lord and Savior, Zacchaeus realized that he had found a treasure more valuable than even the whole world.

> *What good will it be for someone to gain the whole world, yet forfeit their soul? Or what can anyone give in exchange for their soul?*
>
> (MATTHEW 16:26)

Hence, all the wealth he owned was no more the most important for him. That is why he was ready to give half of his wealth to the poor after getting such a great treasure as salvation. So, his earthly wealth was no more primal or of first importance.

Likewise, the Apostle Paul, when he received the Lord Jesus as his Lord and Savior, said in Philippians 3:8:

> *What is more, I consider everything is lost compared to the surpassing greatness of knowing Christ Jesus my Lord, **for whose sake** I have lost all things. I consider them **rubbish** that **I may gain Christ**.*

When he had met Christ, the Apostle Paul stated that of all things he counted but dung or rubbish compared to the salvation bestowed by the Lord.

So, if today we still consider the earthly wealth very precious, we might not realize yet how invaluable the salvation God the Father has given us through the sacrifice of Jesus His only Son. When we understand how precious this salvation is, we will no more consider earthly wealth as something too important.

In his book entitled *The Value of Salvation*, the writer explained that gold became valueless compared to diamond. When we buy a gold ring with a big piece of diamond, the gold will not be put into the account because its value will be too trivial compared to the costly diamond. That was what the Apostle Paul said. When he learned that the salvation through Christ was so invaluable, he counted all earthly wealth and other things only dung or rubbish. When we still consider wealth as something very valuable, we should search deeper to know about the value of the salvation in Christ Jesus.

Second, Zacchaeus said:

...and if I have cheated anybody out of anything, I will pay back four times the amount.

(Luke 19:8b)

Zacchaeus wants to compensate those who have been harmed. He wants to pay all debts and mistakes.

Third, it is stated:

...and if I have cheated anybody out of anything, I will pay back four times the amount.

(Luke 19:8b)

Zacchaeus had made his decision to earn money honestly.

He stated that he would not earn it improperly anymore, because for him to accumulate money was of no importance anymore. So, he did not want to gain money by wrong means.

As it is recorded in Ephesians 4:28:

***Anyone who has been stealing must steal no longer**, but must work, **doing something useful with their own hands**, that they may have something to share with those in need.*

If we truly belong to the fourth type of Christians, we definitely will not earn money by deceiving, blackmailing, stealing, cheating, and other ways that are not in line with God's Word. Even as employees we will not be corruptive, be bribed, receive commission, and the kinds. We also do not feign illness and work leisurely; rather we will work hard and do the best we can.

Zacchaeus wants to carry out his duties as a good tax collector, that is, only doing according to the provisions.

In other words, he "do only legal or rightful jobs." If we have received Christ as our personal Lord and Savior, we will no more seek to find unrightful earnings such as gambling, adultery, cheating, intimidating, usurer, and so on. We want to gain an honest livelihood in accordance with God's Word.

To Pay Tax and to Give Tithe

Luke 20:25 records:

> *He said to them, "**Then give back to Caesar what is Caesar's**, and **to God what is God's**."*

Naturally this is very clear. What we ought to give to Caesar or the government is the tax. We as good citizen should duly pay tax to our government. And honestly this had been the writer's struggle since the year 2000. In the year 2002, the writer wrote a book entitled *Menang Dalam Persaingan Gereja/How to Win in Church Competition*. This is a book about how to apply the modern management in the church so that they can win when competing with activities and entertainments from outside the church. A lecturer of a theological school in Bandung invited the writer to convey the material to his postgraduate students. So the writer did after introducing himself to the students.

During the question and answer session, a student asked, "Pak

Yunus, you are a businessman, aren't you? Do you pay your tax duly?" Wow, the writer was very surprised and shocked by that question. The writer answered apologetically because he had not paid his tax as he should, and he was really embarrassed. That is why the writer has been trying to pay his tax duly since then. Yet there was no opportunity since if we fix our tax, then that tax value could be used by the officials as the basis for setting or correcting our past taxes. And the amount of the correction would be very extensive and possibly the fine would not be in our capacity to pay. Just during the tax amnesty from government in the year 2017, we got the chance to pay tax rightly because the government granted tax amnesty to businessmen who had committed mistakes in their responsibilities to pay tax in the past years. But after the clearance, as we want to start paying tax honestly and rightly, the challenging questions popped up: Should we pay? Why?

Firstly, in 2015 the writer got two honorary acknowledgments. One of the writer's restaurants gained the acknowledgment from the Municipality Government of Bandung as a dutiful taxpayer and the writer personally won the recognition as the third highest taxpayer from the Internal Revenue Service. With those honorary recognitions, the writer and his enterprises have been ranked as a good taxpayer in the sight of the government.

Secondly, our department of finance reminded the writer about the financial condition of the business enterprise: "Sir, this is the condition of our enterprise. You certainly know about the rivalry among restaurants these days. When we raise our tax payment, then here is the list of our restaurants that are threatened to be shut down." Even before we can pay our tax rightly, the possibility of such a big loss was so apparent. How much more when we do pay rightly? So, the writer and his wife struggled whether to pay tax honestly or not. In the end, we decided to pay our tax honestly with the assumption to be able to pay hundred percent by the end of the year.

Thirdly, as it was already reminded by our department of finance, in August 2017 one of the restaurants we owned had to be shut down due to the great loss which could not be recovered. And it was our biggest one, our pride, a two-floor restaurant in Jakarta. The restaurant was often reserved for wedding parties or used for our special company programs we usually arranged there. The site was three thousand square meters, quite spacious, and the restaurant was actually our pride. Again, the writer and his wife struggled whether to continue being honest in paying tax or not. To continue could cause another list of restaurants be shut down too. After the hard struggle, the writer and wife agreed to continue with the decision and keep on paying tax rightly, and although they might have to shut down some more restaurants and only half of them left, they would comply.

Then the Lord reminded the writer to report and to pay tax for a certain transaction. This transaction was done in the past, and if the writer reported it, he would have to pay a very large amount, really huge. At first, we wanted to start anew and closed the old, but the Lord reminded the writer about Zacchaeus. Thus, the writer had to report and to pay the tax which actually could be kept safe and would not be tracked by the Internal Revenue Service.

We keep struggling since the tax is very high. Just early last August, we resolved to pay.

Why are we obliged to pay? There are three reasons.

First, we learn to be obedient, not to gain some compliment. No. If only for a compliment, it would be too expensive since the writer had to pay hundreds of thousand dollars. We only want to obey because the Lord has put on us the responsibility to pay tax. So, we do it.

Second, the writer knows that to be a follower of Christ, there is a price to pay.

Third, the writer used to go to swim with his friends and other entrepreneurs. It has been done for a long time. After swimming, they usually enjoyed breakfast and chatting together. The writer remembered that one day someone among them stated, "Now listen, when we talk about paying tax, none would do it rightly. So, everybody is a thief. Whatever religion they follow, there is no difference. The Christians too are thieves."

Fortunately, his statement stopped there. If it were prolonged, we might hear some comments like this, "Christians, either just members or activists or elders or preachers or Christian writers like Yunus here, are no different. All are thieves." That is why the writer since then always pray to the Lord, "Oh Lord, please help me never to cause Your Name be ridiculed."

When someone talks about Christians, he or she is talking not only about the followers of Christ but also about Christ Himself as Lord of the Christians. So, when somebody says that Christians steal in the issue of taxation, it means he or she directly or indirectly is mocking God for assuming Him of being unable to teach His people to be dutiful taxpayers. For that reason, the writer prayed, "Lord, please enable me to pay tax honestly so that your Name will not be blasphemed."

To Give the Tithe

"Then give back to God what is God's." This concerns our tithe. We ought to give our tithes which actually are our responsibility as Christians. The writer has been faithfully giving his tithes for twenty-five years, but during that time, the writer had stopped practicing it twice. However, about the year 2003, the writer started to give tithes again until now. Through the experience of giving tithes and then stopping it and starting again, the writer can feel the difference between giving and not giving tithe. The writer belongs to those who often encourage others to give their tithes without intending to keep those tithes for himself because the writer is not a minister nor a pastor. So, he will never accept tithes from the congregation for himself, but he do encourage them to practice it as God has promised to bestow a great blessing upon them, as we can read in Malachi 3:10–12:

> *10 Bring the whole tithe into the storehouse, that there may be food in my house. Test me in this, says the LORD Almighty, and see if I* ***will not throw open the floodgates of heaven and pour out so much blessing that you will not have room enough for it****.*
>
> *11 "****I will prevent pests from devouring your crops, and the vines in your fields will not cast their fruit****," says the LORD Almighty.*
>
> *12* ***Then all the nations will call you blessed****, for yours will be a* ***delightful land****," says the LORD Almighty."*
>
> *There are three blessings the Lord promises:*
>
> *First*, the Lord will open the windows of heaven and pour us out a blessing so much that there shall not be room enough to receive it.

Second, the Lord will rebuke all failures so that our efforts and plans would run well.

Third, the most remarkable issue is that we would be a delightful land. So, what is a delightful land? We know that a land consists of people, buildings, facilities, cultures, sites, air, water, community, environment, atmosphere, and so on. The Lord promises to make everything good!

The writer started a business by running a small kiosk at a traditional market, Pasar Kosambi in Bandung, selling peanuts, frying oil, soaps, margarine and butter, and other kinds of food stuff. The writer gave his tithes faithfully and he did not become impoverished by that. On the contrary, his financial condition was raised above the average. Actually, the writer is not the kind of person who likes to tell much about himself and his family. He is afraid of being considered as self-assertive or arrogant. But today, the writer is ready to tell all this frankly as a testimony.

The writer has been blessed with a wonderful wife. They have been married for thirty-five years and had quarreled but less than twenty times during their marriage. The writer has also been blessed with three good children. They are smart and brilliant and have been granted good achievements since their childhood. They are polite and have never caused the family any trouble. The writer's second child was the only Indonesian invited officially to attend Obama's first inauguration as President of the United States of America.

The writer has also been blessed with a grandchild who is very sweet and brilliant. He got an A for all subjects and no B at all. The atmosphere in the writer's home is almost always quiet and restful, with no loud cries of children, and the writer has never seen his three children quarreled with each other. Surely, the Lord has bestowed all the best to the writer and his family!

The writer would like to encourage all of us to give tithes so that we also can experience as Job's who said to the Lord:

> ***My ears had heard of you** but now **my eyes have seen you**.*
>
> (JOB 42:5)

When we listen to God's Word, we only hear. When someone gives a testimony, we only hear. *But God wants us to really experience, not only to hear*, because our faith should be based on what we experience. So, we can say as what the Samaritans said to the woman in John 4:42:

> *They said to the woman, "**We no longer believe just because of what you said**; now **we have heard for ourselves**, and **we know that this man** really is the Savior of the world."*

We ourselves experience what the Lord Jesus says so that we believe and are convinced that God is true.

Some people might say that to be able to experience God's power, it is not necessary by giving tithes. We can feel God's power by experiencing divine healing and other miracles. Indeed that is possible, but when we are healed from our sickness, oftentimes doubt flashed on our mind, "Is it true that we are healed by our prayers? Or are we healed because the doctor is an expert, the medicines he gives are effective, the medical science is sophisticated, and many other common reasons?"

However, when we experience blessings by giving tithes, we will not doubt anymore about God's power since the matter does not agree with the rule of economy, finance, arithmetic, and other scientific calculations. All of them teach us that to be able to own more, we have to spend less. But the Lord through His Word tells us that we have to give our tithes to be richly blessed.

The Other Three Types of Christians Fail, Except the Fourth

In general, the first type of Christians never go to church or go only a few times. The second type of Christians rarely go to church. Sometimes they go, and sometimes they do not because they do not maintain their faith. So, the attendees of the church are the third and the fourth type of Christians. As it has been said previously, *only the fourth type Christians would be saved* or would enter into the Kingdom of Heaven, whereas the other three types of Christians would leave God and their faith would die out.

The writer would like to end this book by quoting Matthew 7:21:

> *Not everyone who says to me, 'Lord, Lord,' will enter the kingdom of heaven, but only the one who does the will of my Father who is in heaven.*

This quotation is taken from a paragraph that consists of three verses. The paragraph was explained by the writer in his book entitled *The Characteristics of God's Children*. So, whoever wants to gain more information about this can simply read the book.

However, here the writer intends only to explain in a simple way the meaning of this verse: "Not everyone who says to me, 'Lord, Lord,' will enter the Kingdom of Heaven"; surely, this part of the verse is very clear that not everyone who goes to church would be allowed to enter into the Kingdom of Heaven nor everyone who sings praises to the Lord. Also not everyone who listens to God's Word would gain access to enter into the Kingdom of Heaven nor everyone who are active in the ministry for the Lord. And not even all who are venerable clergies or preachers or Christian writers like the writer himself could enter into the Kingdom of Heaven for the other part of the verse says, "but only the one who does the will of my Father who is in heaven."

Thus, the key is doing the will of the Father. As long as we do not do this, we most likely would not be allowed to enter into the Kingdom of Heaven. Yes, definitely, the standard is not who cries "Lord, Lord…" nor who attends the church, but who does the will of God.

JESUS
VS
MAMMON

Yunus Ciptawilangga, MBA

Jesus Versus Mammon

As God's children, inevitably we assume that we are sincere followers of Christ. Thus, certainly only the Lord Jesus fills the deepest of our hearts. But is it really so? Is it true that only the Lord Jesus reigns in our hearts? Let's all together examine ourselves.

Let us read two passages—John 4:7–42 and Mark 5:1–20 as follows:

John 4:7 When a Samaritan woman came to draw water, Jesus said to her, "Will you give me a drink?"

8 (His disciples had gone into the town to buy food.)

9 The Samaritan woman said to him, "You are a Jew and I am a Samaritan woman. How can you ask me for a drink?" (For Jews do not associate with Samaritans.)

10 Jesus answered her, "If you knew the gift of God and who it is that asks you for a drink, you would have asked him and he would have given you living water."

11 "Sir," the woman said, "you have nothing to draw with and the well is deep. Where can you get this living water?

12 Are you greater than our father Jacob, who gave us the well and drank from it himself, as did also his sons and his livestock?"

13 Jesus answered, "Everyone who drinks this water will be thirsty again,

14 but whoever drinks the water I give them will never thirst. Indeed, the water I give them will become in them a spring of water welling up to eternal life."

15 The woman said to him, "Sir, give me this water so that I won't get thirsty and have to keep coming here to draw water."

16 He told her, "Go, call your husband and come back."

17 "I have no husband," she replied.

Jesus said to her, "You are right when you say you have no husband.

18 The fact is, you have had five husbands, and the man you now have is not your husband. What you have just said is quite true."

19 "Sir," the woman said, "I can see that you are a prophet.

20 Our ancestors worshiped on this mountain, but you Jews claim that the place where we must worship is in Jerusalem."

21 "Woman," Jesus replied, "believe me, a time is coming when you will worship the Father neither on this mountain nor in Jerusalem.

22 You Samaritans worship what you do not know; we worship what we do know, for salvation is from the Jews.

23 Yet a time is coming and has now come when the true worshipers will worship the Father in the Spirit and in truth, for they are the kind of worshipers the Father seeks.

24 God is spirit, and his worshipers must worship in the Spirit and in truth."

25 The woman said, "I know that Messiah" (called Christ) "is coming. When he comes, he will explain everything to us."

26 Then Jesus declared, "I, the one speaking to you—I am he."

The Disciples Rejoin Jesus

27 Just then his disciples returned and were surprised to find him talking with a woman. But no one asked, "What do you want?" or "Why are you talking with her?"

28 Then, leaving her water jar, the woman went back to the town and said to the people,

29 "Come, see a man who told me everything I ever did. Could this be the Messiah?"

30 They came out of the town and made their way toward him.

31 Meanwhile his disciples urged him, "Rabbi, eat something."

32 But he said to them, "I have food to eat that you know nothing about."

33 Then his disciples said to each other, "Could someone have brought him food?"

34 "My food," said Jesus, "is to do the will of him who sent me and to finish his work.

35 Don't you have a saying, 'It's still four months until harvest'? I tell you, open your eyes and look at the fields! They are ripe for harvest.

36 Even now the one who reaps draws a wage and harvests a crop for eternal life, so that the sower and the reaper may be glad together.

37 Thus the saying 'One sows and another reaps' is true.

38 I sent you to reap what you have not worked for. Others have done the hard work, and you have reaped the benefits of their labor."

Many Samaritans Believe

39 Many of the Samaritans from that town believed in him because of the woman's testimony, "He told me everything I ever did."

40 ***So when the Samaritans came to him, they urged him to stay with them, and he stayed two days.***

41 And because of his words many more became believers.

42 They said to the woman, "We no longer believe just because of what you said; now we have heard for ourselves, and we know that this man really is the Savior of the world."

Mark 5:1 They went across the lake to the region of the Gerasenes.

2 When Jesus got out of the boat, a man with an impure spirit came from the tombs to meet him.

3 This man lived in the tombs, and no one could bind him anymore, not even with a chain.

4 For he had often been chained hand and foot, but he tore the chains apart and broke the irons on his feet. No one was strong enough to subdue him.

5 Night and day among the tombs and in the hills he would cry out and cut himself with stones.

6 When he saw Jesus from a distance, he ran and fell on his knees in front of him.

7 He shouted at the top of his voice, "What do you want with me, Jesus, Son of the Most High God? In God's name don't torture me!"

8 For Jesus had said to him, "Come out of this man, you impure spirit!"

9 Then Jesus asked him, "What is your name?"

"My name is Legion," he replied, "for we are many."

10 And he begged Jesus again and again not to send them out of the area.

11 A large herd of pigs was feeding on the nearby hillside.

12 The demons begged Jesus, "Send us among the pigs; allow us to go into them."

13 He gave them permission, and the impure spirits came out and went into the pigs. The herd, about two thousand in number, rushed down the steep bank into the lake and were drowned.

14 Those tending the pigs ran off and reported this in the town and countryside, and the people went out to see what had happened.

15 When they came to Jesus, they saw the man who had been possessed by the legion of demons, sitting there, dressed and in his right mind; and they were afraid.

16 Those who had seen it told the people what had happened to the demon-possessed man—and told about the pigs as well.

17 ***Then the people began to plead with Jesus to leave their region.***

18 As Jesus was getting into the boat, the man who had been demon-possessed begged to go with him.

19 Jesus did not let him, but said, "Go home to your own people and tell them how much the Lord has done for you, and how he has had mercy on you."

20 So the man went away and began to tell in the Decapolis how much Jesus had done for him. And all the people were amazed.

From these two passages, we read that both groups of society responded differently toward the presence of the Lord Jesus.

The first group, the community in Samaria, pleaded the Lord Jesus to stay with them:

So when the Samaritans came to him, they urged him to stay with them, and he stayed two days.

(JOHN 4:40)

On the other hand, the second group which was in Gerasa asked the Lord Jesus to leave them, even urged Him to do so:

Then the people began to plead with Jesus to leave their region.

(MARK 5:17)

Why did the Samaritans and the Gerasenes in the passages above responded differently even contradictory toward the presence of the Lord Jesus?

Let us study them together.

The Samaritans:

- The Lord Jesus did a miracle by stating to the Samaritan woman about her husband:

John 4:16 He told her, "Go, call your husband and come back."

17 "I have no husband," she replied. Jesus said to her, "You are right when you say you have no husband.

18 The fact is, you have had five husbands, and the man you now have is not your husband. What you have just said is quite true."

19 "Sir," the woman said, "I can see that you are a prophet.

- The Samaritan woman went back to town to tell the people about the presence of the Lord Jesus and the miracle He had done:

John 4:28 Then, leaving her water jar, the woman went back to the town and said to the people,

29 "Come, see a man who told me everything I ever did. Could this be the Messiah?"

- The Samaritans asked Jesus to stay with them:

So when the Samaritans came to him, they urged him to stay with them, and he stayed two days. (John 4:40)

The Gerasenes:

- The Lord Jesus performed a miracle by casting away one legion (4000–6000) evil spirits from a demon-possessed man and made the person sane again:

Mark 5:8 For Jesus had said to him, "Come out of this man, you impure spirit!"

9 Then Jesus asked him, "What is your name?"

"My name is Legion," he replied, "for we are many."

When they came to Jesus, they saw the man who had been possessed by the legion of demons, sitting there, dressed and in his right mind; and they were afraid. (Mark 5:15)

- They who tended the pigs went to town to tell about the presence of the Lord Jesus and the miracles He had done:

Those tending the pigs ran off and reported this in the town and countryside, and the people went out to see what had happened.

(MARK 5:14)

- The people coming out of the town could see the result of the miracles the Lord Jesus had done to the possessed man who was already dressed and sane:

When they came to Jesus, they saw the man who had been possessed by the legion of demons, sitting there, dressed and in his right mind; and they were afraid.

(MARK 5:15)

- The people who witnessed those miracles confirmed what the Lord Jesus had done:

Those who had seen it told the people what had happened to the demon-possessed man—and told about the pigs as well.

(MARK 5:16)

- The Gerasenes pleaded the Lord Jesus to leave them:

Then the people began to plead with Jesus to leave their region.

(MARK 5:17)

From the above description, we can see that what happened in both areas was miraculous, and obviously the miracles Jesus did in Gerasa were far more powerful than those in Samaria. The Gerasenes too saw the result of the miracles which truth was reconfirmed by the people who witnessed them.

The question is, why then did the people of Gerasa urge the Lord Jesus to leave their area?

The answer is found in verse 16:

Those who had seen it told the people what had happened to the demon-possessed man—and told ***about the pigs*** *as well.*

The people of Gerasa saw the power of the Lord Jesus. They also believed that the Lord Jesus was not just anybody, yet they urged Him to leave them because they felt that His presence had caused them material loss, the death of their pigs!

Nowadays we live in a world where the offer of all kinds of objects and services is huge and very intense, completely different from the days of Abraham, for example. During Abraham's lifetime, a fatted calf was considered the most luxurious food. Purple was the most luxurious clothing, and gold was the most luxurious jewelry. Hence when people of Abraham's contemporary had gained the three items, they were satisfied as those were the only ultimate luxuries they could achieve. Also, since at that time electricity was not yet invented, human activities then were relatively shorter and there was almost no nightlife.

Contrary to that era, the price for one meal today is from one US dollar to five thousand US dollars either lunch or dinner.

A man's shirt is available from two US dollars up to two thousand US dollars.

A lady's dress attire is from twenty US dollars up to twenty thousand US dollars or even more.

A wristwatch is from ten US dollars up to million dollars.

As a consequence, we will never feel that we have enough money, for when we are able to buy an item of worth X, sure enough another better item of worth X + Y catches our eyes. Likewise, when we are able to buy that item of worth X + Y, it turns out that there is another better stuff of worth X + Y + Z, and so on.

When we newly own a motorcycle, we might think that if we could own a car, we would be very happy and contented because we need not be drenched with rain and we would be more comfortable. When we are able to buy a small car, we feel so happy… Now, are we satisfied? Maybe, though just for a short time, but later on we will feel dissatisfied as we look at other people around us and see the advantages of the other cars. Suppose we own a bigger car, will it not be better? Then we get the bigger car. Are we satisfied? No, not yet. We want to have a car with a softer suspension. We replace our car with a sedan. Are we satisfied then? No, not yet, because we want a car of better prestige. We want a Mercedes. Then, when we buy a Mercedes of a C class, we will want to change it again with an E class, then an S class, and so on and on. Will we be satisfied now at last? No, not yet, because we still want another car of a more prestigious brand.

Likewise with our house, fancy bags, clothing, travels, and other things. Consequently, we will never feel that we have enough money. Instead, we will always feel we lack money because there are still so many unfulfilled desires. Consequently, we become stingy!

We restrain from giving our tithe because we think that at the moment, we are still short of money. We think that many desires are not yet fulfilled. We also become stingy and restrain from helping our relatives and fellowman because we feel that what we own today is still lacking and we need more money to satisfy our desires.

That is why preaching about money becomes a very sensitive issue and, if possible, would be avoided by some of God's servants.

A senior pastor once told me that he was very careful when he needed to mention about money in his sermons since every time the issue of money was brought up, there were always protests and people offended. Why would the congregation be offended? This happens when despite the fact that the congregation assume themselves as children of God, deep in their hearts mammon is the god they worship. Therefore, whenever the issue of mammon was touched, the church felt it as a blow aimed at her idol, the mammon.

People today idolize mammon. The value of an individual seems to rely upon his or her properties. Therefore, people respect others who are richer. When the richer peoples talk, they gain more attention, and their opinions are more respected. They are given better status and facilities, as well as better positions. My friend said that even at home, some parents appreciate their rich children more than their poorer ones, notwithstanding the behavior of the latest are nobler. Nowadays honoring parents seems to be proportional to how much money the children give them, so my friend added. All is measured by money. Kindness and good manners seem to have no value, much less faith and obedience to God.

This happens in the family too; some wives have almost no respect for their husbands just because the husband is unable to earn a lot of money. Some wives even dare to despise their husbands just because they earn more than the husbands. As children of God, the wives knew that they must submit to their husbands, but because they can make more money, they assume themselves to be in a higher position than their husbands.

Some churches cannot detach themselves from materialism and the feeling of discontentment. That's why some churches continually improve and enlarge their buildings, adding thereby the facilities or conveniences, but do not feel like needing to support the ministries and the pastors in rural areas.

What are the characteristics of Christ's followers referring to money?

Let us read Luke 19:8 as follows:

But Zacchaeus stood up and said to the Lord, "Look, Lord! Here and now I give half of my possessions to the poor, and if I have cheated anybody out of anything, I will pay back four times the amount."

When Zacchaeus became a follower of Christ, he did two things that show his attitude toward money:

1. **Money is not primary.**

> *Lord! Here and now I give half of my possessions to the poor.*

Why could Zacchaeus gave away half of his possessions? It was because he considered his wealth and properties not primary. Why could he be like that? Since Zacchaeus had found what was far more valuable and that was the Lord Jesus.

2. **Pay debt and earn money in the right way.**

> *...if I have cheated anybody out of anything, I will pay back four times the amount.*

When Zacchaeus put the Lord Jesus as most important in his heart, not again did he want to earn money in a manner against God's Word.

As God's children living in an age when mammon (wealth and riches) is idolized like today, it is necessary for us to actually check whether we are sincere followers of the Lord Jesus. Is it true that The One who reigns in our hearts is Christ Jesus our Lord? Who knows whether our confession that we are followers of Christ is but lip service, while in reality it is mammon that reigns in our hearts? When mammon is primary in our lives, our thought patterns or concepts are filled with materialism and consequently our behavior is materialistic.

As children of God, it is very dangerous for us when mammon becomes primal in our lives, for we will expel our Lord Jesus Christ from our hearts once we feel that we suffer some loss as followers of

Christ. We feel that our position is hindered, we cannot hold certain positions, nor take some particular project, nor marry a certain person, and so on. At that instance, we will become like the people of Gerasa—we would urge the Lord Jesus to go out of our hearts.

Furthermore, as described in the book *The Rapture, Fulfillment of: The Signs in the Sky, the Festivals in Summer, and the Parable of the End Times*, at the end times, we would be challenged to choose whether to remain as devout followers of the Lord Jesus and take the risk of losing all our wealth and riches or to leave the Lord Jesus to convert to the other belief accepting the mark 666. When mammon reigns in our hearts, we would definitely choose to leave the Lord Jesus rather than to lose our earthly wealth.

Hebrews 6:4–6 makes it clear that God's children who has fallen away as a renegade cannot turn back to be God's child. Therefore, we should not mess our faith:

> *4 It is impossible for those who have once been enlightened, who have tasted the heavenly gift, who have shared in the Holy Spirit,*
>
> *5 who have tasted the goodness of the word of God and the powers of the coming age*
>
> *6 and who have fallen away, to be brought back to repentance. To their loss they are crucifying the Son of God all over again and subjecting him to public disgrace.*

In this span of life still left and granted for us to live, let us learn to be sincere followers of Christ.

Let us pay our tithes:

Malachi 3:8 "Will a mere mortal rob God? Yet you rob me." But you ask, "How are we robbing you?" In tithes and offerings.

9 You are under a curse—your whole nation—because you are robbing me.

10 "Bring the whole tithe into the storehouse, that there may be food in my house. Test me in this," says the Lord Almighty, "and see if I will not throw open the floodgates of heaven and pour out so much blessing that there will not be room enough to store it.

11 I will prevent pests from devouring your crops, and the vines in your fields will not drop their fruit before it is ripe," says the Lord Almighty.

12 "Then all the nations will call you blessed, for yours will be a delightful land," says the Lord Almighty.

Let us help our brethren:

Anyone who does not provide for their relatives, and especially for their own household, has denied the faith and is worse than an unbeliever.

(1 Timothy 5:8)

This is how we know who the children of God are and who the children of the devil are: Anyone who does not do what is right is not God's child, nor is anyone who does not love their brother and sister.

(1 John 3:10)

If anyone has material possessions and sees a brother or sister in need but has no pity on them, how can the love of God be in that person?

(1 John 3:17)

Whoever claims to love God yet hates a brother or sister is a liar. For whoever does not love their brother and sister, whom they have seen, cannot love God, whom they have not seen.

(1 John 4:20)

Let us obtain money in the right way:

Anyone who has been stealing must steal no longer, but must work, doing something useful with their own hands, that they may have something to share with those in need.

(Ephesians 4:28)

"Caesar's," they replied. Then he said to them, "So give back to Caesar what is Caesar's, and to God what is God's."

(Matthew 22:21)

THE GREAT COMMISSION

Yunus Ciptawilangga, MBA

THE GREAT COMMISSION

The writer is convinced that as God's children, we must have heard about the Great Commission. Before the Lord Jesus ascended into heaven, He conveyed a final message which was very important for all humanity. That message was the Great Commission from our Lord Jesus to the believers. This Great Commission is recorded in the Bible, among others, in the following:

> *Matthew 28:19 Therefore go and make disciples of all nations, baptizing them in the name of the Father and of the Son and of the Holy Spirit,*
>
> *20 and teaching them to obey everything I have commanded you. And surely I am with you always, to the very end of the age.*

The Great Commission clearly assigned us to go to spread the Gospel, the Good News of the Lord Jesus Christ, and the assignment or mission is reconfirmed in Ephesians 6:15:

And with your feet fitted with the readiness that comes from the gospel of peace.

(Please read the writer's book entitled *The Victorious People*).

As God's people, we certainly want to carry out this Great Commission of our Lord Jesus. So how would we take into consideration the significance of this Great Commission and then act upon it, exerting every effort to spread the Gospel to people around us?

Be the Salt and the Light

Jesus claimed His disciples to be the salt of the earth and the light of the world:

You are the salt of the earth. But if the salt loses its saltiness, how can it be made salty again? It is no longer good for anything, except to be thrown out and trampled underfoot.

You are the light of the world. A town built on a hill cannot be hidden.

(Matthew 5:13–14)

Salt is to give taste, which means that as disciples of Christ, we should be able to give some taste or sense of life in Christ to our environment and even to the world. All of our behavior, our thinking, or our lifestyle should be able to influence people around us, in our environment. We should give some taste or sense of the Gospel to our families and our environment so that they could taste or experience the blessings and the love of Christ in their lives.

To be the light of the world means that our lives should reflect Christ because Christ is the light of the world, as stated in John 9:5:

While I am in the world, I am the light of the world.

A life that reflects Christ means that our lives should be like Christ's, as stated in Romans 8:29:

For those God foreknew he also predestined to be conformed to the image of his Son, that he might be the firstborn among many brothers and sisters.

When we become the light of the world, people will see the image of Christ in our lives, and living as the light of the world, we would illuminate our environment and provide enlightenment or insights about the eternal salvation and the truth.

Exemplary

When we evangelize, we do not do it just verbally or only by our words, but also by our deeds since those we evangelize do not only hear but also see. In short, we do not just talk, but become an example too for them as the Lord Jesus had done, according to John 13:15:

I have set you ***an example*** *that you should do as I have done for you.*

The same lifestyle is shown by the Apostle Paul, written in 2 Thessalonians 3:9:

> *We did this, not because we do not have the right to such help, but in order to make ourselves **a model** for you to follow.*

The Apostle Paul also gave the same advice to Titus, for example, in Titus 2:7:

> *In everything set them **an example** by doing what is good. In your teaching show integrity, seriousness.*

Similarly, he gave the same advice to Timothy, in 1 Timothy 4:12:

> *Don't let anyone look down on you because you are young, but set **an example** for the believers in speech, in life, in love, in faith and in purity.*

Then in Titus 2:1–10 too, it is expressed even more clearly how people should behave:

> *Titus 2:1 You, however, must teach what is appropriate to sound doctrine.*
>
> *2 Teach the older men to be temperate, worthy of respect, self-controlled, and sound in faith, in love and in endurance.*
>
> *3 Likewise, teach the older women to be reverent in the way*

they live, not to be slanderers or addicted to much wine, but to teach what is good.

4 Then they can urge the younger women to love their husbands and children,

5 to be self-controlled and pure, to be busy at home, to be kind, and to be subject to their husbands, so that no one will malign the word of God.

6 Similarly, encourage the young men to be self-controlled.

7 In everything set them an example by doing what is good. In your teaching show integrity, seriousness

8 and soundness of speech that cannot be condemned, so that those who oppose you may be ashamed because they have nothing bad to say about us.

9 Teach slaves to be subject to their masters in everything, to try to please them, not to talk back to them,

10 and not to steal from them, but to show that they can be fully trusted, so that in every way they will make the teaching about God our Savior attractive.

Furthermore, although we evangelize, we ourselves are still learners, which means that we continually have to learn more to be like Christ. So, it is a lifelong learning process. Therefore, we should not wait until we are perfect before we evangelize, because we can never be perfect. Indeed, evangelizing would spur us to become better disciples of Christ.

Jerusalem: Our Family

Then when we read Acts 1:8, regarding the Great Commission, it is said:

> *But you will receive power when the Holy Spirit comes on you; and you will be my witnesses in Jerusalem, and in all Judea and Samaria, and to the ends of the earth.*

The phrase "in Jerusalem, and in all Judea and Samaria, and to the ends of the earth" could perhaps be considered as one of our guidance today for evangelism. Although we do not live in the vicinity of Jerusalem, we can apply the principle of this phrase symbolically, where Jerusalem symbolizes our family, children, wife, and husband.

To make every endeavor for all members of our family to become God's people is the ministry God assigned us, written in Deuteronomy 6:

> *5 Love the Lord your God with all your heart and with all your soul and with all your strength.*

> *6 These commandments that I give you today are to be on your hearts.*

7 Impress them on your children. Talk about them when you sit at home and when you walk along the road, when you lie down and when you get up.

8 Tie them as symbols on your hands and bind them on your foreheads.

9 Write them on the doorframes of your houses and on your gates.

The verses above clearly state that we have to teach the Word of God repeatedly to our children and become doers of the God's Word in our lives.

What is God's purpose here?

Malachi 2:15 explains that God requires of a family a divine offspring, children of God:

Has not the LORD made them one? In flesh and spirit they are his. And why one? Because he was seeking ***godly offspring****. So guard yourself in your spirit, and do not break faith with the wife of your youth.*

In fact, in Malachi 2:10–16, the Lord God emphasized that besides a divine offspring, He demanded loyalty between the married couple, between husband and wife.

The Lord God very seriously desires that every descendant of God's children becomes a divine offspring. God even planned to kill Moses because Moses had neglected to circumcise his son, which means that Moses neglected to bring his child to become God's child and God's people.

> *At a lodging place on the way, the Lord met Moses and was about to kill him.*
>
> *(Exodus 4:24)*

From the above verse, as God sought to kill Moses, we realize that the task to make each one of our children become a divine child or God's child is a serious matter demanded by God. Please read more about this in the book *Our Major Ministry* and *A People Prepared for the Lord.*

However, some of God's children prefer to evangelize people outside their family circle rather than members of their own family. Why? Because they meet with difficulties in evangelizing members of their family. In fact, quite many complained that when they told about the Gospel, their family members tended to be stubborn, unyielding, and some other reasons. If we consider deeply, one of the reasons is because *we ourselves are not yet doers of the Word*, thence when we tell the Gospel, arguments and resistance arise in the hearts of the people we evangelize.

Our family members have been living with us so that they know how we live our lives. Consequently, when we evangelize them, they will *grumble* or say in their hearts, "Ah, that is nice speech, but his/her behavior does not reflect it."

Therefore, we should be doers of the Word, be the salt of the earth and the light of the world, as exemplified in Peter 3:1–2:

> *Wives, in the same way be submissive to your husbands so that, if any of them do not believe the word,* ***they may be won***

over without words by the behavior of their wives*, when they see the purity and reverence of your lives.*

The verse above explains that a wife could win her husband even without words, only through her pure and pious lifestyle, and this is the expression of doing the Word.

Thus it is clear the Great Commission demands that we should be doers of the Word, the salt of the earth and the light of the world, so that we would be able to make disciples of Christ of all nations, which can be started with our own family members.

Judea: Our Big Family

When all members of our family have become disciples of Christ—husband, wife, and children—we can expand our evangelism *throughout Judea.* What is Judea? Judea is the province where Jerusalem is located. So if Jerusalem is to be the symbol for our family, then Judea symbolizes our extended family: our parents, brothers and sisters, relatives, and even our in-laws.

It is not easy to evangelize our big family. Yet if we have become doers of the Word, this would be the rootstock or provision for us to make our big family disciples of Christ.

Further in 1 John 3:17 we read:

If anyone has material possessions and sees a brother or sister in need but has no pity on them, how can the love of God be in that person?

This verse tells us that we must help our brothers or fellowmen who are in need. From the writer's observations and experiences within his big family, he noticed that one of the obstacles which stagnated the evangelism among them was because we did not want to help our relatives who were in difficulties. Oftentimes we were still reluctant to spend our money, our time, and our energy to help them. We might love God and our brothers/fellowmen, but we love mammon and our possessions more. (Please read the writer's book entitled *Jesus Versus Mammon*). The writer witnessed that when God's children in his big family were willing to help other members of the family by offering their time, money, resources, and efforts, then evangelism went smoothly. Even without too many verbal explanations, they who did not believe could be won for Christ. When we help our relatives, to the extent that they can solve their problems, those family members who still do not believe yet in the Lord Jesus Christ would be more openhearted because *they can see and feel God's love through us, His children.*

> *In the same way, let your light shine before others, that they may see your good deeds and glorify your Father in heaven.*
>
> *(MATTHEW 5:16)*

Samaria: Our Neighbor

Then *Samaria*, the neighboring province next to Judea, symbolizes our neighbor(s). Our neighbors are not merely neighbors in the actual sense, but can also be our business partners, our friends, and even our acquaintances. So that is our picture of Samaria. There is a very clear example in the Bible of how we can evangelize or on what basic reason do we evangelize our neighbors or our business associates. This happened when the Lord Jesus was on the way back from Judea to Galilee, passing through Samaria. He stopped by a well and sat down and then asked for some water from a Samaritan woman:

When a Samaritan woman came to draw water, Jesus said to her, "Will you give me a drink?"

(JOHN 4:7)

The Samaritan woman said to him, "You are a Jew and I am a Samaritan woman. How can you ask me for a drink?" (For Jews do not associate with Samaritans).

(JOHN 4:9)

In the end we know that not only the Samaritan woman was saved, but the entire population living in that town too. How could it be like that? Because Jesus *did not discriminate against anyone*, whether the person is a Jew, a Samaritan, or any other individual considered to be of low standing. Likewise, when we treat everyone as God's glorious creation and make no distinction among people, whether they are poor or rich, of good position or not, from any race, then we would be able to evangelize them.

The same thing happened to Peter. Peter began to reach out to other nations outside the Jewish people when he realized that God did not discriminate against any man:

Acts 34 Then Peter began to speak: "I now realize how true it is that ***God does not show favoritism****.*

35 But accepts men from every nation who fear him and do what is right."

To the Ends of the Earth

Furthermore, we can expand our evangelism "to the ends of the earth" or "unto the uttermost part of the earth." If we can evangelize our own family by being doers of the Word and can evangelize our big family without being attached and tied to our wealth or properties, which means that we are willing to help others and consider every man equal in the eyes of God, equally valuable, hence we can also evangelize a wider environment. We can make disciples of Christ of all nations.

Conclusion

Then the writer wants to close this writing with a personal experience. In the past, the writer belonged to those who were not very active in the church because during the year 1980–2000, he focused more in learning five major religions. Thus, he turned down many offers to join in Christian ministries or activities. During that period of his study, he believed that the most important ministry was to serve our family. However, oftentimes conflicts arose in his mind whether or not he was too selfish, as he was concerned only with his own family and cared less about others until at some point in the year 2006. At that time his eldest daughter had completed her study in Australia. She planned to continue her education in China to learn Mandarin, for her fiancé spoke Mandarin daily in his family, while we spoke Indonesian in our family. If she did not learn Mandarin, she would not be able to communicate well with her husband's family in the future. A few days later, after she arrived in Beijing, he and his wife, with their two other children, visited her there in order to see and know for themselves the condition of the campus, the environment, and her colleges. Thus, they could understand better when later she would call them up or communicate with other means.

During their stay in Beijing, they were assisted by a local guide, Mrs. Ellis, who could speak Indonesian. Since their purpose there was only to see the campus and its environment, they did not have any particular activities. They just walked to the mall and had lunch and dinner and a chat with Mrs. Ellis.

It turned out that Mrs. Ellis was a Christian but had not gone to church for quite a while since the church was a bit far, and her son also complained that he was excommunicated after his friends knew that his mother was a Christian. Her husband was a public prosecutor and non-Christian. From their conversations, the writer got to know that Mrs. Ellis' family was not so harmonious, and she asked a lot of questions about how they bring up their children and edify their family. Therefore, the writer told her more about the experiences of how to rear and edify a family and so on. Relatively he himself did not talk much about the Gospel, just told her what they used to do in their family.

Then the writer remembered the fourth day they were in Beijing as Mrs. Ellis drove them to the airport. Before parting, she said to the writer, "Sir, after all our conversations and as I watch your family, I'm going to attend the church again."

Until now the writer still feel the thrill of amazement when he recall this particular event, and the experience affirms him that it is not always necessary to talk much in evangelizing. Instead, a sincere and harmonious family could also be a means to evangelize. And since then he became more confident of what he has been doing is right, so he keeps on making every effort to provide sufficient time to take care of his family, to educate and edify.

Finally, we have to yield the people we have evangelized to the Lord because only by God's power and grace could they be saved. The best thing we can do is to pray for them, witness to them, and live the Christian life in front of them as an example for them, because it is God who makes them grow, as stated 1 Corinthians 3:6 in the following:

I planted the seed, Apollos watered it, but God made it grow.

The Writer

Drs.Yunus Ciptawilangga, MBA

Education: 1984—Bachelor of English Language
1993—Master of Business Administration
Profession: Entrepreneur in restaurants and technology of information

CPSIA information can be obtained
at www.ICGtesting.com
Printed in the USA
LVHW081518230822
726674LV00015B/720

9 781400 330522